FAMILY, JUSTICE, AND DELINQUENCY

Recent Titles in
Contributions in Family Studies

A Social History of American Family Sociology, 1865–1940
Ronald L. Howard; John Mogey, editor

Women in the Family and the Economy: An International Comparative Survey
George Kurian and Ratna Ghosh, editors

Revolutions in Americans' Lives: A Demographic Perspective on the History of
Americans, Their Families, and Their Society
Robert V. Wells

Three Different Worlds: Women, Men, and Children in an Industrializing Community
Frances Abrahamer Rothstein

Family and Work: Comparative Convergences
Merlin B. Brinkerhoff, editor

Child-Rearing and Reform: A Study of the Nobility in Eighteenth-Century Poland
Bogna Lorence-Kot

Parent-Child Interaction in Transition
George Kurian, editor

The Dutch Gentry, 1500–1650: Family, Faith, and Fortune
Sherrin Marshall

Migrants in Europe: The Role of Family, Labor, and Politics
Hans Christian Buechler and Judith-Maria Buechler, editors

A History of Marriage Systems
G. Robina Quale

Feeding Infants in Four Societies: Causes and Consequences of Mothers' Choices
Beverly Winikoff, Mary Ann Castle, Virginia Hight Laukaran, editors

The Reconstruction of Family Policy
Elaine A. Anderson and Richard C. Hula, editors

FAMILY, JUSTICE, AND DELINQUENCY

Brenda Geiger
and **Michael Fischer**

Foreword by Hans Toch

Contributions in Family Studies, Number 16

GREENWOOD PRESS
Westport, Connecticut • London

Library of Congress Cataloging-in-Publication Data

Geiger, Brenda.
    Family, justice, and delinquency / Brenda Geiger and Michael
  Fischer ; foreword by Hans Toch.
        p.   cm.—(Contributions in family studies, ISSN 0147–1023;
  no. 16)
    Includes bibliographical references and index.
    ISBN 0–313–29458–5 (alk. paper)
    1. Child rearing—United States. 2. Child rearing—Israel.
  3. Children's rights. 4. Family. 5. Justice. 6. Juvenile
  delinquency. 7. Kibbutzim. I. Fischer, Michael. II. Title.
  III. Series.
  HQ769.G375   1995
  649′.1—dc20   94–27943

British Library Cataloguing in Publication Data is available.

Library of Congress Catalog Card Number: 94–27943
ISBN: 0–313–29458–5
ISSN: 0147–1023

First published in 1995

Greenwood Press, 88 Post Road West, Westport, CT 06881
An imprint of Greenwood Publishing Group, Inc.

Printed in the United States of America

The paper used in this book complies with the
Permanent Paper Standard issued by the National
Information Standards Organization (Z39.48–1984).

10 9 8 7 6 5 4 3 2 1

Copyright Acknowledgments

The authors and publisher gratefully acknowledge permission to use the following:

Excerpts from *Causes of Delinquency* by Travis Hirschi. Copyright 1969.
University of California Press, Berkeley, CA. Used by permission of Travis Hirschi.

Excerpts from *A Theory of Justice* by John Rawls. Copyright 1971. Harvard
University Press. Used by permission of Harvard University Press, Cambridge, MA.

To Adina, Danielle, Arielle, Avital, and Eliana

Our Beloved Children

Contents

Foreword by Hans Toch   ix

Acknowledgments   xiii

Introduction   xv

1.   The Original Position   1

2.   Children's Rights   13

3.   Children's Fate in Western Society   27

4.   The Kibbutz Egalitarian Society   37

5.   Social Conformity and Deviance: Kibbutz versus Nuclear-Family Children   47

6.   Moral Autonomy   73

7.   Implications for Americans   89

Appendix A: U.N. Declaration of the Rights of the Child   103

Appendix B: Self-Report Research Instrument   105

Appendix C: Questionnaire   109

Notes   115

Bibliography   121

Index   139

Foreword

As the twenty-first century impends we discover ourselves engulfed in social problems, which are recited to us with monotonous and disturbing regularity, and with no apparent effect. One reason that we feel unable to escape from the morass that we are in, is that the solutions our pundits and politicians propose, strike other pundits and politicians as utopian or ineffectual, unworkable or unaffordable, and at extremes, as inhumane, unprincipled, and unethical.

A case in point is the question of what to do about the decline of the nuclear family, and the indisputable consequences attendant to this decline. In parts of our metropolitan areas the majority of children are born out of wedlock—often to underage mothers—and such children are reared on welfare and in poverty. An alarming proportion of the children underperform in schools, become unemployable, fall prey to substance abuse, and embark on careers of precocious and checkered delinquency, or worse.

As I write, the President and the congress are engaged in one of their periodic campaigns to discourage the proliferation of welfare-dependent families. The formula being discussed combines discontinuance of child support payments with vocational training for mothers, and provides accessibility to child care. However, controversy about the details of the proposal endangers its enactment. And even if such were not the case, most observers agree that what is proposed is too modest or too expensive, or both.

Some activists on the right of the ideological spectrum have argued that we should start out by declaring most unwed mothers ill-equipped for the delicate task of raising their children. The next step that is envisaged is unclear, but appears to consist of the establishment of a network of orphanages or foster care homes, which is to be privately supported in unspecified ways. Predictably, most critics on the left have classed this proposal as nightmarish, retrogressive, and totalitarian.

Against this sort of backdrop come Brenda Geiger and Michael Fischer with their enticing book, which returns the debate to fundamentals because this book rests soundly on theoretical underpinnings. Geiger and Fischer start with Rawls' seminal *Theory of Justice*, which they apply to the question of how we can do justice for children. As example, Geiger and Fischer propose that parents or those acting in *loco parentis* be required to show that they can make choices for children and that the latter "would choose for themselves had they enjoyed adult capacities"; and be "guided by their children's wishes and preferences, as long as these are not irrational"; and that they accord children fundamental "primary goals" when their wishes and preferences are unknown. This means that one does not provide children with unfettered freedom, but "helps (them) obtain wealth, opportunity, self-respect, and any other primary good that would stimulate the development of their capacity for autonomous choice."

The core of this book is an exploratory comparative study of the perspectives of children raised collectively in Israeli kibbutzim with those of comparable children raised in conventional homes. The study relied on an instrument devised by Hirschi, the premier American criminologist, who argues that delinquency results from attenuated attachment to significant others—which is in turn a product of dysfunctional families. Geiger and Fischer's survey is admittedly modest, but the results of their study are dramatic. Responses to one question after another suggest that youths who are raised in a combinatory arrangement that includes family and communal socialization evolve a strong bond to prosocial peers that exercises constructive restraints on conduct. Such findings are congruent with those of other research that shows kibbutz graduates are high on moral development when compared with subjects otherwise raised.

Geiger and Fischer don't argue that collective child rearing is superior to socialization that occurs in well-functioning families. Their commitment to the nuclear family is attested to by the dedication of their book to *five* much-loved children of their own. Moreover, their view of child-care arrangements is guarded: one topic in chapter 7 reads "Daycare for Infants: Dilemma or Disaster?" They are aware of the results of our wholesale reliance on substandard nursery schools and ill-trained (though heroic) child-care workers, struggling against odds to make up for indifferent parenting. Geiger and Fischer assert that there are innovative options we have not yet explored; options that do not throw out the baby of the family with the bathwater of its dysfunctions.

Among the themes of the book is one that Geiger and Fischer have previously dealt with, in a monograph on socialization and crime. They point out that recruitment into delinquency can be reversed by changing the polarities of formative experiences. Lousy families drive youths into the arms of predelinquent peers who share their primitive dispositions and asocial attitudes. This confluence leads to an incestuous reinforcement of delinquent dispositions. The challenge we face is to find a constructive alternative to negative peer influence.

In their books, Geiger and Fischer propose that the answer lies in exposing youngsters during their formative years to social microcosms based on collaborative problem solving, sharing, interdependence, collective responsibility, and distributive justice. The kibbutz offers a model that suggests that this can be done.

Geiger and Fischer search for a civilized formula for raising children to become law-abiding citizens. Drawing on thinking that ranges from philosophy to criminology, psychology, and educational theory they suggest that we can achieve justice and equity by treating children justly and equitably and expecting them to pass on this heritage to their own children. They imply that where today we have cycles of violence, we can tomorrow have cycles of responsible citizenry.

I can only conclude by reassuring the prospective reader that this book is socially responsible and consistently humane. It is also important because it contains ideas that are worthy of consideration and deserving of support.

Hans Toch
Albany, New York
July, 1994

Acknowledgments

Our sincere appreciation to Dr. Hirschi and Dr. Reese for their vital assistance and direction. Our thanks to Arthur Smith for the patience that only a true philosopher could have. Special thanks to William Schwarz for sharing with us his knowledge in computer science.

Introduction

Eli Levi, 20 years old, was born in an Israeli kibbutz. He grew up in the children's house sharing his toys, feelings, and thoughts with his peers. While working in the various branches of agriculture, he finished high school. Then he enlisted in the Israeli Defense Forces (I.D.F.) to become a paratrooper. During a weekend furlough he decided to go to Jaffa to visit his cousin Mordechai. Coming off the bus, Eli saw Mordechai standing at a street corner of the neighborhood and talking to other *chach-chachim*.[1] Mordechai was also in his twenties, but he did not finish high school, let alone fifth grade. His mother was never home when he came back from school and could not watch him. She had to clean houses in order to support the family. His father has been for many years partially disabled, unemployed, and often drunk. He would yell at Mordechai and tell him to stop wasting his time with school nonsense, to go to work instead and make money. Sometimes, he would even beat his son with a belt. Mordechai also never really worked. He is a delinquent known to the police. He did not enlist in the I.D.F and cannot find a job. He likes to visit Eli and listen to his stories about kibbutz cooperation and equality. He often wonders whether things would have been different had he been raised in the kibbutz.

Like Mordechai, many children in Israel and America are neglected, battered, and stripped of their self-respect. Their ties to their parents are weak or broken. Normless, they are indifferent to the consequences of their actions or to the fate of their victims. The abyss of drugs and delinquency is open to them.

In this book, several institutions affecting children are examined within a Rawlsian perspective of justice as fairness. The first principle of justice requires equality of liberty for all, the second allows for socioeconomic inequalities only if they improve the prospects of the least advantaged under conditions of fair equality of opportunity. The goal of this book is to examine which child-rearing practices, nuclear family or kibbutz, are more consistent with the principles of justice as fairness, better protect the rights and interests of children, and allow for greater moral growth and maturity so as to minimize the incidence of abused, neglected, and anomic children.

Parents are imagined to be going back through the four-stage sequence of Rawls' original position. This hypothetical contractual situation allows for the adoption of the perspective of justice during deliberations. Indeed, the skill of judgment with respect to justice involves moving back and forth between the original position and real-life situations. The movement from theory to practice in the process of reflective equilibrium is also of this type.

In chapter 1, the basic concepts of Rawls' *Theory of Justice* are examined. These include the original position, the characteristics of the parties in it, and the models for choosing the principles of justice.

In chapter 2, the principle of liberty is applied to children. Not possessing the same mental and physical capabilities as adults, children need to be protected. They cannot enjoy liberty rights as adults do. Questions of paternalistic agency arise, such as, who will act in the best interests of children? Do parents have absolute authority over their children, and what kind of authority is to be delegated to parents or to anyone acting in *loco parentis*?

In chapters 3 and 4, the nuclear and kibbutz families are situated within their broader socioeconomic contexts. The fate of nuclear-family children within our present day capitalist economy is examined in chapter 3. Great inequalities of wealth and power among families have far-reaching consequences affecting children's education and development. Rawls' program of socioeconomic reform, which aims at narrowing down these inequalities, is examined, including the claim that fair equality of opportunity cannot be achieved as long as the family exists as the primary child-rearing and economic unit.

In chapter 4, a more egalitarian community, the kibbutz, is examined. In this society principles similar to Rawls' have been implemented. However, in the kibbutz the nuclear family does not exist as an economic institution. The welfare of children does not depend on their parents' socioeconomic status. Children's education is the responsibility of the whole community. Children share communal resources, including its parenting capabilities. Although they no longer sleep at the children's house, but at their parents' home, children spend, from infancy, a major portion of their waking hours in nurseries, schools, and after-school programs, and participate in various communal activities.

In chapters 5 and 6, self-report research conducted in Israel in 1986 and several other studies provide empirical evidence for more theoretical claims about justice as fairness with the goal of finding out which child-rearing structure, nuclear or kibbutz, allows for autonomous moral development of least advantaged children.

In the concluding chapter, the implications that flow from a wealth of research findings on kibbutz communal child-rearing practices are examined in relation to American families. As community linkages weaken and parents entrust their children more and more to nurseries, preschools, day care, schools, and after-schools, the problem of finding quality care and education is becoming more urgent. The kibbutz educational system sheds light on how to stimulate intellectual and moral growth of all children, including the most disadvantaged among them.

FAMILY, JUSTICE, AND DELINQUENCY

Chapter 1

The Original Position

In this preliminary chapter, the main concepts of Rawls' original position are analyzed as well as the characteristics of the individuals in this situation and the principles of justice they choose.[2] Rawls (1971) revives the notion of social contract as an alternative to classical utilitarianism.[3] Under the constraints imposed by the hypothetical original position, self-interested individuals are to agree unanimously on the principles that will regulate the major institutions of their society, that is, its basic structure (Rawls, 1971). These principles would allow us to evaluate socioeconomic institutions in order to determine whether the rewards and burdens related to roles and positions are fairly distributed. These principles will represent the final court of appeal for any claim of change or reform aimed at regulating inequalities and preventing injustice.

When judging the fairness of an institution and the inequalities it allows, underlying principles and resultant distribution must be considered. The first criterion of evaluation is whether rights are equally distributed. The second is whether it is rational for the least-advantaged representative individuals of a practice to accept its inequalities. If the condition and prospects of the least advantaged are improved under these inequalities, then the practice may be considered fair; otherwise, it may not.

The original position is a decision-making procedure setting up fair conditions and procedural constraints for choosing principles of justice. One set of constraints consists of formal conditions that the principles of justice must satisfy (Rawls, 1971). These principles must be general in formulation, universal in application, and public. They will impose a transitive ordering on competing claims and override the demands of law, custom, and self-interest.

THE VEIL OF IGNORANCE: CONSTRAINT ON KNOWLEDGE

Another set of constraints imposes limitations on knowledge. The contracting parties are assumed to be under a thick veil of ignorance, which is the key condition of the original position (Rawls, 1971). They forget all personal characteristics: whether they are intelligent or stupid, honest or criminal. They no longer know their talents and capabilities, social class, and socioeconomic status. When reflecting about their society, they do not know its cultural level or sociopolitical situation. They suffer from total amnesia with respect to particular facts. Concealing these facts is deemed necessary to achieve symmetry between parties as free and equal moral persons and to prevent them from tailoring principles to their own advantage (Rawls, 1980).[4]

The only particular fact about society that the veil of ignorance does not conceal is that society is subject to the circumstances of justice. Rawls (1971) interprets this fact, as Hume (1978) does, in terms of moderate scarcity. In *A Treatise of Human Nature*, Hume (1978) argues that if natural and social resources were unlimited, justice would be superfluous. He cites air and water as such examples. "This we may observe with regard to air and water, tho' the most valuable of all external objects; and may easily conclude, that if men were supplied with everything in the same abundance . . . justice and injustice would be equally unknown among mankind" (p. 495).

CHARACTERISTICS OF THE INDIVIDUALS IN THE ORIGINAL POSITION

Lacking preferences, motives, and goals in life, one may wonder why the individuals in the original position would want to deliberate about justice. More assumptions are, therefore, required to motivate these individuals. Rawls (1980) adds the notion of life plans and the theory of primary goods in order to provide a model of the person which, when combined with the model of the original position, would yield principles of justice.

Rawls' Model of the Person

Rawls (1980) characterizes a moral person by two capacities related to two desires. The first capacity is an effective sense of justice combined with the desire for adopting the standpoint of justice. He also argues that the desire to act on moral principles and the desire to express one's nature as a free and moral person are "practically speaking" the same desires. The second characteristic of a moral person is to be a purposeful agent who forms, revises, and rationally pursues his conception of the good. Rawls adopts here Royce's conception of the person who "may be regarded as a human life lived according to a plan" (1971: p. 408). This plan would include the coherent goals of a conscious person. If this plan is rational, the conception of one's good is also rational.

Although the veil of ignorance conceals the parties' specific plans, it does not prevent them from knowing that they have such life plans, since it is the capacity to choose one's ends that make individuals people, whatever the ends chosen. A third interest thus moves the parties, namely, the desire to protect and advance their plans, whatever they turn out to be. In contrast to the two previous "highest order desires," this last desire is a "higher," and not a "highest" order desire, and thus ranks below the two other desires (Rawls, 1980).

These desires are still too abstract to provide the required impetus for addressing the problem of justice. Thus, Rawls further assumes that the individuals in the original position have preferences for certain primary goods defined in terms of what is rational for people to want in order to carry out their life plans. These goods include rights, liberties, opportunities, power, wealth, and the social basis of self-respect. They are social and under society's direct control, whereas beauty, intelligence, and wit are natural goods and are only indirectly influenced by social institutions (Rawls, 1971). Justice as fairness is mainly concerned with the distribution of primary social goods and not with the distribution of natural goods. Self-respect is the most important primary good. Its social basis is defined as:

> Those aspects of basic institutions which are normally essential if individuals are to have a lively sense of their own worth as moral persons and to be able to realize their higher-order interests and advance their ends with zest and self-confidence. (Rawls, 1980: p. 526)

In the well-ordered society, self-worth and how one values others could not be based on income, wealth, or power, but on the public affirmation of equal citizenship (Rawls, 1971). Otherwise, some would be more worthy of respect than others only because they are richer or more powerful. Self-respect is connected to the notion of the person as an end in itself. It reflects the idea that one's plans are worth pursuing. A social dimension is also added to this personal aspect of self-respect in the notion of mutual respect between people. It may thus be argued that the right of self-respect and equal concern is not the product of the contract, but its condition. This right is owed to people as moral persons and possessed by anyone who can deliberate about justice (Dworkin, 1975).

Theory of Primary Goods and Human Nature

Rawls (1971) seems to have derived the concept of primary goods from premises about human nature and its needs and wants. Several objections could be raised to such derivation. First, the psychological assumption that everyone always wants more primary goods may be false. Rawls is aware of this possibility: "To be sure, the theory of these goods depends on psychological premises and these may prove incorrect" (1971: p. 260). Second, a cultural bias is introduced into what was supposed to be value free. For instance, a priest who takes the vow of poverty may want only a minimum amount of primary goods to survive. His higher spiritual goals would be violated by the desire for an ever-increasing amount of wealth and power (Wolff, 1977).

To avoid these problems, Rawls revises his assumptions. In a later article, "Kantian Constructivism in Moral Philosophy: Rational and Full Autonomy" (1980), the concept of moral persons and their highest-order desires becomes the new basis for the preference for primary goods. "Primary goods are singled out by asking which things are generally necessary as social conditions and all-purpose means to enable human beings to realize and exercise their moral powers and to pursue their final ends" (Rawls, 1980: p. 526). In this manner, psychological and sociological theories no longer have an impact on the notion of a person. However, they remain invaluable for the application of principles of justice to social institutions (Rawls, 1980).

Autonomy

The individuals in the original position are assumed to be rationally autonomous and to act solely on motives of pure reason (Rawls, 1980). They are not bound by any antecedent principle of right and are a self-originating source of principles. Rawls does not, however, reject self-interest as a motivating force as long as it is constrained within the limits set by the veil of ignorance. Self-interest focuses on the primary goods that the veil of ignorance does not obscure, and since these goods originate from our moral personality, self-interest does not conflict with morality. It is rational to want primary goods and to value them, whatever our final ends turn out to be. Our moral personality, self-interest, and rationality become linked by the common denominator of primary goods. It is in our interest as moral and rational persons to desire primary goods in order to achieve our final ends.

Benevolence and altruism are excluded as superfluous notions, and replaced by a weaker assumption of mutual disinterest. Although the individuals in the original position may be self-interested, they are neither interested in other persons' interests nor envious. They are mutually disinterested. This characteristic, combined with the veil of ignorance, aims to achieve the same goal as the all-knowing sympathetic, benevolent, and impartial observer under the utilitarian doctrine. In both cases, specific constraints force the contracting parties to consider the good of others as well as their own:

> Moreover the theory of justice assumes a definite limit on the strength of social and altruistic motivation. It supposes that individuals and groups put forward competing claims, and while they are willing to act justly, they are not prepared to abandon their interests. (Rawls, 1971: p. 281)

For Rawls, justice is distinct from benevolence, altruism, and sympathy. It regulates all feelings. Rawls' and Hume's positions on this subject are antithetical. Hume (1978) argues that if there were no selfishness or scarcity, justice would not be needed: "Encrease to a sufficient degree the benevolence of men, or the bounty of nature, and you render justice useless, by supplying its place with much nobler virtues, and more favourable blessings" (Hume, 1978: pp. 494–495). By contrast, for Rawls, justice would be needed even if no one were selfish.

Rationality

The contracting parties adopt the principles of rational choice and deliberative rationality as self-evident (Rawls, 1971). These require that one choose:

1. The most efficient means to reach one's goals.

2. The most inclusive life plans.

3. Among the various alternatives open, the one that is most likely to occur and that would allow for the realization of one's most fundamental desires.

4. Finally, rational persons commit themselves only to principles that are reasonable and can be adhered to. "They will not enter into agreements they know they cannot keep, or can do so only with great difficulty" (Rawls, 1971: p. 145).

Social Cooperation

The desire for social cooperation is another assumption of *A Theory of Justice*. The parties realize that they are not self-sufficient. However, their common desire for an ever-increasing amount of primary goods creates conflicts of interest that raise the problem of justice and require the search for a fair solution to the distribution of such goods.

Summary

Under the veil of ignorance, the individuals in the original position are characterized as free, equal, and rational. They are self-interested but not envious. To maximize the possession of primary goods, they decide to cooperate in order to choose the principles that ought to regulate the basic institutions of their society.

TWO MODELS OF CHOICE: RATIONAL RECONSTRUCTION AND THE BARGAINING MODELS

Rawls' first model of choice is the rational reconstruction model. To justify their moral and social convictions about justice, the individuals in the original position look for the principles that would form the deep structure of their moral reasoning. Rawls (1980) assumes that there is such a structure, just as there is a depth grammar underlying speech:

> What justifies a conception of justice is not its being true to an order antecedent to and given to us, but its congruence with our deeper understanding of ourselves and our aspirations, and our realization that, given our history and the traditions embedded in our public life, it is the most reasonable doctrine for us. (p. 519)

Principles of justice are justified when they are congruent with one's shared moral and social convictions about what is right. They must have intuitive appeal and be accepted by everyone after reflection. Intuition acts as a warning light to indicate lack of congruence. In such a case, adjustments must be made at the level of principles and judgments until a best fit may be found. "Justification is a matter of the mutual support of many considerations, of everything fitting together into one coherent view" (Rawls, 1971: p. 21).

Rawls (1971) uses a complex version of inductive justification in moral reasoning. Within this pattern, principles of morality are justified only if they are congruent with accepted moral judgements, and moral judgements are in turn justified only if they are congruent with those principles. This circularity is, however, not vicious since justification of both principles and particular judgments consists in their being brought into agreement, or reflective equilibrium (Gewirth, 1978). Rawls (1971) describes this process as follows:

> By going back and forth, sometimes altering the conditions of the contractual circumstances, at others withdrawing our judgments and conforming them to principle, I assume that eventually we shall find a description of the initial situation that both expresses reasonable conditions and yields principles which match our considered judgments duly pruned and adjusted. (p. 20)

Rawls (1971) argues that although the process of reflective equilibrium would lead all rational persons to agree after "due reflection," any increase in sophistication and knowledge available under the veil of ignorance could produce a different type of agreement. On the other hand, he (1980) also argues that the combination of the models of the original position, of the person, and of the well-ordered society, yield a single theory of justice. The first argument allows for the possibility of a changing conception of justice: the second at least seems to deny it. However, this issue we need not face since our concern is only with the application of Rawls' theory to the institutions affecting children.

Rational Reconstruction Model

The first principle found at the core of one's moral and social convictions is the principle of equal liberty. "Each person is to have an equal right to the most extensive total system of equal basic liberties compatible with a similar system of liberties for all" (Rawls, 1971: p. 302).

The second principle is that of fair equality of opportunity with the difference principle as its clause. "Social and economic inequalities are to be arranged so that they are both (a) to the greatest benefit of the least advantaged—and (b) attached to offices and positions open to all under conditions of fair equality of opportunity" (Rawls, 1971: p. 83).

Rawls (1971) distinguishes between a general and a special conception of justice. The former depicts a society experiencing severe socioeconomic hardships such as hunger and starvation. Under these circumstances, liberty loses significance and is often sacrificed for other socioeconomic goods deemed prerequisite for the effective exercise of liberty.

However, when society has reached a certain level of economic prosperity, as is the case under the special conception of justice, liberty assumes priority. The principles of justice become lexically ordered so that the principle of equal liberty must be satisfied before principles regulating other socioeconomic goods are applied. Therefore, "liberty can be restricted only for the sake of liberty" (Rawls, 1971: p. 302). Rawls' rationale for this priority is that once a certain level of well-being has been reached, every member of society, even those who belong to the lowest socioeconomic rung, will after reflection realize the importance of liberty and prefer it to any other socioeconomic good.

It may be argued that from the assumptions that the individuals in the original position prefer certain goods, among which liberty is included, and that they want as many primary goods as they can get from social cooperation, Rawls could not have inferred the priority of liberty. He must have already assumed that in the original position people prefer liberty to other primary goods (Hare, 1975; Wolff, 1977).

Bargaining Model

The bargaining model, which is the second model for choosing the principles of justice, reduces the role of intuition to a minimum. In this model, the parties in the original position know that their society enjoys moderate scarcity of goods and bargain for principles that would allow them to obtain a maximum amount of primary goods.

The parties are also assumed to be nonenvious, and would therefore be ready to accept an unequal distribution of goods if their conditions were improved regardless of what others gain. To the contrary, had they been envious, they would never accept such inequality, even at the expense of losing extra advantage, since their main concern would be that others do not get more than they do.

Another assumption of the bargaining model is that because the individuals in the original position are not risk takers, they adopt the maximin as a bargaining strategy. This pessimistic rule of choice under uncertainty recommends to assume the worst and to imagine a society in which an enemy assigns everyone a place in its design. It requires that one always choose the best among the worst alternatives.

Rawls' arguments for the maximin are (1) since under the veil of ignorance one cannot estimate the probability of being in any specific social-economic position, and (2) since the individuals in the original position are not risk takers, it would be irrational for them to gamble the minimum guaranteed by the maximin for uncertain advantages. With respect to the first reason, risk taking in the original position appears to be just as rational as non-risk taking; consequently, the assumption that those in the original position are not risk takers is what supports the maximin.[5] The adoption of the maximin leads to the choice of the difference principle for the distribution of socioeconomic goods other than liberty and, therefore, to Rawls' theory of justice. Change the initial assumption, and one arrives at a different conception of justice. Rawls (1971) is well aware of this possibility since he calls his theory *A Theory of Justice* rather than *The Theory of Justice*.

Bargaining Process

The maximin tells the parties to choose the best among the worst possible outcomes. Given that the individuals in the original position have life plans and that they want to maximize the amount of primary goods they could obtain from social cooperation, their indifference curve is the same. It would thus be irrational for them to settle for anything less than strict equality, or an average expected amount of primary goods. The principle of equal liberty and the first clause of the principle of fair equality of opportunity are first agreed upon. The latter stipulates that those with similar abilities should have equal chances of attaining specific positions regardless of their socioeconomic condition.

However, there is no reason why strict equality should be the final choice. In a three-step deliberation process, the parties in the original position choose the difference principle as a legitimate upper bound.

Strict equality in the distribution of socioeconomic goods is first agreed upon. "This state of affairs provides a benchmark for judging improvements" (Rawls, 1971: p. 62). However, the parties realize that there may be inequalities that could make everyone better off. So in a second step of reasoning they stipulate that if there are inequalities that make everyone better off they should be accepted. But the phrase "inequalities that make everyone better off" is ambiguous since there are many possible criteria that could satisfy this claim. Thus, in the third step of their deliberations the parties in the original position adopt the criterion of the least advantaged:

> In order to make the principle regulating inequalities determinate, one looks at the system from *the standpoint of the least advantaged representative man* [italics added for emphasis]. Inequalities are permissible when they maximize, or at least contribute to, the long-term expectations of the least fortunate group. (Rawls, 1971: p. 151)

The problem of justice thus becomes that of identifying the least advantaged representative individuals of an institution. The index of primary goods allows for their location. Intercomparisons are made in terms of primary goods: rights, opportunities, power, income, wealth, and self-respect.

The maximin agreed upon is therefore the lexical difference principle:

> In a basic structure with n relevant representatives, first maximize the welfare of the worst-off representative man; second, for equal welfare of the worst-off representative man, maximize the welfare of the second worst-off representative man, and so on until that last case which is, for equal welfare of all the preceding n-1 representatives, maximize the welfare of the best-off representative man. (Rawls, 1971: p. 83)

In its simpler form, this principle reads, "social and economic inequalities are to be arranged so that they are both (a) to the greatest benefit of the least advantaged and (b) attached to offices and positions open to all under conditions of fair equality of opportunity" (Rawls, 1971: p. 83).

A BIAS FOR JUSTICE: ANOTHER ASSUMPTION

A much debated issue is whether Rawls should have added the additional premise that in the original position the contracting parties have a bias for justice, that is, that they are not only are rational, self-interested, and mutually disinterested, but also have a somewhat realized sense of justice. Those who reject this additional premise argue that the contracting parties commit themselves to justice on the basis of self-interest and self-interest alone. They accept the original position as the strategy most consistent with self-interest and choose principles and policies that would protect and advance it.

Rawls' bias (1971) against intuition shows that he favors the bargaining model over the rational reconstruction model. Because of problems of subjectivity in weighing first principles, Rawls hopes to reduce the role of intuition to a minimum, while not believing it can be "eliminated entirely" (1971, p. 41). He argues that this can be partially achieved by reference to the original position and through the proposed lexical ordering. In the bargaining model his goal is to show that under the procedural constraints of the original position, self-interested and mutually disinterested individuals would adopt principles of justice without abandoning their prudential reasoning. In fact, the principles of justice can be derived from the bargaining model only when that model is combined with the model of rational reconstruction via the process of reflective equilibrium. And, in fact, Rawls does use these models together.

If, however, the moral assumptions of the rational reconstruction model were not added to the bargaining model, there would be nothing to prevent the most advantaged individuals from rejecting the difference principle once the veil of ignorance is removed. Rather than formulating policies that reduce their power, they could offer the least advantaged the same deal Nozick (1974) proposes:

> Look, better endowed: you gain by cooperating with us. If you want our cooperation you'll have to accept reasonable terms. We suggest these terms: We'll cooperate with you only if we get *as much as possible.* That is, the terms of our cooperation should give us that maximal share such that, if it was tried to give us more, we'd end up with less. (p. 195)

This bargain would certainly discriminate against the least advantaged, but Rawls' proposal may be conceived as discriminating against the most advantaged and, therefore, as no more legitimate. Rawls (1971) objects that the best-off have no reason to complain about the difference principle because without such principle, social cooperation would be impossible. Once this principle is established, the smooth cooperation with the worst-off would make the best-off realize that the stable society in which they live has eliminated crime, suicide, anomie, and other forms of social disintegration. Therefore, the difference principle is also in the best interest of the most advantaged.

Furthermore, as Miller (1975) argues, the most advantaged would eventually outgrow their greed and realize that the cost endured because of the difference principle is only transitory. "For the rebellion of despondency of a representative member of a deposed upper class might be a passing phase; he might grow out of his old felt needs and become more or less satisfied with what the difference principle allots him" (p. 221).

Finally, Rawls (1971) argues that commitment to justice does not result from deliberation in the original position only, but from daily experience with just institutions. Doubtless, problems remain with the bargaining model in moving from the veiled to the open society. Doubtless, some will drop the difference principle—but those committed to justice will uphold it.

In the rational reconstruction model, the contracting parties have moral convictions and moral intuitions to support the principles agreed upon via the process of reflective equilibrium. In the well-ordered society, individuals have a developed sense of justice. The ideals of reciprocity and fraternity, which are related to the difference principle, bind the people of the well-ordered society into a community. Thus, when they move back to the original position, the contracting parties may not have a developed sense of justice, but the potentiality for its development is already present.

The best-off accept the difference principle because they already have a bias for justice. In a sense this is also implicit in the assumption of nonenvy, although it is not argued here that Rawls has associated a bias for justice with nonenvy. Because of this bias, the contracting parties are able to reach fairness through ideal role-taking and to internalize the ideals of reciprocity and fraternity. The most advantaged remain committed to the difference principle even when they discover that they are more talented because they empathize with the less fortunate and actively want to share with them their resources. "The difference principle, however, does seem to correspond to a natural meaning of fraternity: namely, to the idea of not wanting to have greater advantages unless this is to the benefit of others who are less well off" (Rawls, 1971: p. 105).

The Rawlsian individuals consider their talents and contributions to society as common assets for the benefit of all. This is the ideal of those who understand that it is only in a social union that they could self-actualize and be given the respect and dignity that is owed to every human being. Thus, the principles of justice are in reflective equilibrium with the considered moral judgments of those who already have a bias for justice. Rawls may or may not hold this. The evidence is mixed. In any case, appropriate moral assumptions about human nature must be added to the bargaining model.

Chapter 2

Children's Rights

Once the principles of justice are chosen, the contracting parties move to the second stage of the original position. The veil of ignorance is being progressively removed and additional information is available. The goal of this stage is to promulgate the most effective and just constitution. For this purpose, the country's geographical location, its political and socioeconomic structure, its history, and its cultural level are additional facts revealed to the contracting parties.

Once constitutional powers and basic rights are formulated, the parties move to the third stage of the original position, its legislative stage, and apply the second principle of justice. The full range of people's beliefs and interests becomes known.

At the fourth stage of the original position, the veil of ignorance is totally removed and all information that would have created bias and distortion in earlier stages is revealed (Rawls, 1971). The contracting parties regain their place in society and then apply rules and policies to particular cases.

In this book, the contracting parties are imagined to be going through this four-stage decision-making procedure. They want to make sure that no matter what happens to them, death, insanity, divorce, impatience, or lack of parenting ability, the social institutions they have chosen will stimulate the intellectual and moral development of their most important resource: their children.

Under Rawls' theory (1971), children belong to the class of individuals that ought to receive the full protection of justice because they possess potential although not yet realized moral capacities. "One should observe that moral personality is here defined as a potentiality that is ordinarily realized in due course. It is this potentiality which brings the claims of justice into play" (p. 505). Therefore, at the constitutional convention stage, the parties ought to apply the principle of liberty to the legal institutions affecting their children.

CHILD'S LEGAL STATUS WITHIN THE ANGLO-AMERICAN TRADITION

A main characteristic of the Anglo-American legal tradition is the restriction of the child's liberty, which seems to constitute an infringement upon the first principle of justice. Children do not enjoy the same rights or constitutional safeguards as adults. They have diminished civil and criminal responsibility. Children are subjected to the will of their parents, who have the right to raise and nurture them as they see fit. This right has been defined as "sacred," as a matter of "natural law," and as an "inherent natural right." It has been protected with the same fervor as the rights to life, liberty, and the pursuit of happiness (Hafen, 1976: p. 616).

For example, Supreme Court case *Parham v. J. L. and J. R.*, U.S. 99, S. Ct. 2493 (1979) reaffirmed the presumption of parental beneficence by upholding the commitment to a mental institution of an unwilling child who had been "volunteered" by his parents. This child was not given a fact-finding hearing, which would have accompanied any involuntary adult civil commitment to a mental institution.[6] The rationale of the court is presented by Chief Justice Berger:

> We conclude that our precedents permit the parents to retain a substantial, if not the dominant role in the decision, absent a finding of neglect or abuse, and that the traditional presumption that the parents act in the best interests of their children should apply. (*Parham v. J. L. and J. R.*, cited in Cohen, 1980: p. 354)

The child's disadvantaged position becomes even more evident with the increasing number of dysfunctional and disintegrated families and the state's hopeless attempt to compensate for their breakdown.

THE NUCLEAR FAMILY IN THE 1990s

Industrialization, urbanization, and bureaucratization have permanently altered our communities. In the 1990s, a gemeinschaft with strong extended family ties and strong norms and social controls no longer exists in the Western world (Bell, 1973; Toffler, 1971; Warren, 1978). The extended family has been scattered: the nuclear family is weakened and sometimes pulverized. For example, in the United States the number of divorces in relation to the number of marriages has risen from 10.8 percent in 1916, to 25.8 percent in 1960, and to 50 percent in 1991.[7]

Structural changes in well-functioning homes are also taking place. Whereas in 1955, 60 percent of all households in the United States consisted of a working father, a housewife mother, and two or more school-age children, by 1985 only 7 percent of the households fit this profile (Davis & McCaul, 1991: p. 4). In 1992, 59.9 percent of wives with husbands present and with a child under six years of age at home were working in comparison to 18.6 percent in 1960.[8] Similarly, 56.7 percent of wives with husbands present and with a child one year or younger at home were working in 1992, in comparison to 30.8 percent in 1975.[9] In 1989, 57.4 percent of separated women with children at home less than six years of age worked, and 70.5 percent of divorced women with children at home less than six years of age worked.[10]

RISING INCIDENTS OF CHILD ABUSE AND NEGLECT

The weakening of the nuclear family has been accompanied by a sharp increase in the reported incidents of child abuse and neglect. From 1978 to 1987, the rate of reports of such incidents has more than tripled.[11] In 1991, 2,695,010 children were reported to be abused or neglected in the United States.[12] Each year more than three million children witness physical, mental, or sexual attacks of their mothers by their partners.[13] In the frequently cited Strauss and Gelles household survey, 12.6 percent of children in U. S. households were found to experience severe to very severe acts of violence (*Healthy Children*, 1988: p. 171). Sexual abuse has also been found to be one of the fastest-growing forms of crime against children (*Healthy Children*, 1988: p. 171). The very young, those under three years of age, are overrepresented among the victims (*Healthy Children*, 1988: p. 173; Sabotta & Davis, 1992).

> Using a very conservative sexual abuse *prevalence* rate of 5 percent obtained from various community surveys, Finkelhor and Hotaling estimate that something on the order of 150,000 to 200,000 new cases of child sexual abuse occur each year. (*Healthy Children*, 1988: p. 172)

The exact extent of child abuse and neglect or its impact on youth's development is hard to determine.[14] While doctors and teachers are required to report suspected cases of abuse and neglect, any victim not brought to a doctor or not attending school cannot be identified. Jason (1984) estimates that even child homicide is underreported in the Untied States by at least 20 percent. Many deaths that are reported as resulting from Sudden Infant Death Syndrome (SIDS), accidents, and other kinds of fatalities are really murders. Although exact statistics are not known, many studies indicate that abused and neglected children often suffer long-term damage and are likely to become abusive parents themselves.[15]

> The effects of child abuse and neglect are cumulative. Once the
> developmental process of a child is insulted or arrested by bizarre child
> rearing pattern, the scars remain. One should not be surprised, then, to
> find that the large majority of delinquent adolescents indicate that they
> were abused as children. (Helfer & Kempe, 1976: pp. XVII–XVIII)

> The problem is clearly not just one of *physical* battering. Save for the
> children who are killed or endure permanent brain damage . . . the most
> devastating aspect of abuse and neglect is the permanent adverse effects
> on the developmental process and the child's emotional well-being.
> (Helfer & Kempe, 1976: p. XIX)

When compared to children of the same background, sexually abused and
neglected children from lower-middle-class intact families and from families
receiving Aid to Families with Dependent Children (AFDC) were found to
suffer marked cognitive and behavioral deficiencies (Reyone, 1993).
Maltreated children in both groups had lower grades, were more likely to
repeat a grade, and were in greater need of placement in special classes.[16]
Abused children reported to have committed twice as many delinquent acts
and were arrested twice as often as youngsters who had not been maltreated
(Allen-Hagen & Sickmund, 1993). Individuals who had been sexually
abused as children were also found to suffer from sexual dysfunction and
depression in adulthood (Beitchman et al., 1992).

The problems of runaways (*Drug Abuse and Prevention Programs for
Youth*, 1991; Powers, Eckenrode, & Jaklitsch, 1990), homeless (Heflin &
Rudy, 1991; Levitan & Schillmoeller, 1991), throwaways (Moses & Kopplin,
1992), pushouts (Dorrell, 1992), bag kids, latch-key children,[17] persons in
need of supervision (PINS), and "Rat Pack" youth (Hawkins, 1985) continue
to grow. Over one million children are estimated to run away from home
each year.[18] Approximately one million children drop out of school each
year (Dorrell, 1992). These children are three and a half times more likely to
be arrested than high school graduates (Schorr, 1988). Runaways are
vulnerable to drug abuse, gangs, and prostitution (Arthur & Erickson, 1992;
Rafferty & Shinn, 1991; Whitbeck & Simons, 1990).

The government has responded to the phenomena of abuse, neglect, and
delinquency by multiplying agencies supposed to help least advantaged
children. One of these bureaucratic networks, the juvenile justice system, is
examined next.

JUVENILE JUSTICE SYSTEM AND *PARENS PATRIA* DOCTRINE

The power of the state to interfere coercively in the lives of youths is linked to the right of parents to raise their children. Under the *parens patria* doctrine, the state is authorized to "act in *loco parentis* for the purpose of protecting the property interests and the person of the child" (*In re Gault*, cited in Cohen, 1980: p. 568). The establishment of the juvenile court in 1899 was motivated by lofty ideals, which are reflected in Judge Mack's comment:

> That is the conception that the State is the higher parent; that it has an obligation, not merely a right but an obligation, toward its children; and that is a specific obligation to step in when the natural parent, either through viciousness or inability, fails so to deal with the child that it no longer goes along the right path that leads to good, sound, adult citizenship. (Judge Mack, cited in Duffee, Hussey, & Kramer, 1978: p. 265)

In 1990, juvenile courts nationwide disposed of 1,265,000 delinquency cases.[19] This represents a 146.1 percent increase over the number of cases the juvenile courts disposed of in 1960,[20] while during this time interval the U. S. population grew by only 38.3 percent.[21] In 1989, there were 624,597 admissions of juveniles to public facilities and 141,907 admissions to private facilities.[22] Nevertheless, the effectiveness of the juvenile justice system is being questioned. Do judges, social workers, custodial staff and maintenance staff, who are after all professional strangers, act in the child's best interest?

The President's Commission on Law Enforcement and Administration of Justice (1967) and the National Advisory Commission on Criminal Justice Standards and Goals (1976) expressed doubt about a system that may generate juvenile delinquency:

> The evidence suggests that official response to the behavior in question may initiate processes that push the misbehaving juveniles toward further delinquent conduct, and, at least, make it more difficult for them to re-enter the conventional world. (President's Commission, 1967: p. 417)

Labeling theorists (Becker, 1973; Lemert, 1972) explain how all the steps of juvenile delinquency proceedings, from arrest to the status degradation ceremony at trial and later to imprisonment, contribute to the juvenile's loss of identity and yield secondary deviance not ordinarily following the primary delinquent act:

The process of making the criminal, therefore, is a process of tagging, defining, identifying, segregating, describing, emphasizing, making conscious and self-conscious . . . . The person becomes the thing he is described as being. (Tannenbaum, 1938: pp. 19–20)

Furthermore, institutionalization, by subjecting the youth to the socialization process of institutions, has the most destructive impact (Goffman: 1961). Sykes (1958), Clemmer (1958), and Messinger (1969) have spoken of the phenomenon of prisonization. Inmates deprived of basic human necessities such as freedom of movement, privacy, and sex, turn to each other or upon each other when they form groups with antisocial norms. The newly arrived delinquent, whether placed in the institution because of joyriding or homicide, must quickly learn the ropes in order to avoid victimization.[23]

GAULT: SUPREME COURT PROTECTION FOR JUVENILES

The Supreme Court decision *In re Gault*, 387 U.S. 1, 87 S. Ct. 1428 (1966) confronted the objection that the juvenile justice system, which deprives youths of their constitutional rights, fails in its rehabilitative task. Free of fundamental constitutional inhibitions, this system does not reduce crime, and the classification of juveniles as delinquents rather than criminals has not been successful in preventing them from being labeled criminals.

The Supreme Court, therefore, stressed the importance of protecting children's liberty rights: "Neither the Fourteenth Amendment nor the Bill of Rights are for adults alone" (*In re Gault*, cited in Cohen, 1980: p. 566), and took judicial notice of the harsh and massive curtailment of liberty juveniles face when placed in juvenile facilities. It held that juvenile delinquency adjudication proceedings violated the due process clause of the Fourteenth Amendment. The court, thus, demanded for the youth provision of protections included in the Fifth and Sixth Amendments, namely, the right to counsel, protection against self-incrimination, the right to confront witnesses and cross-examination, timely notice, and specificity of charges during those proceedings (Kamisar, 1981: app. A, p. 3).

The Significance of *Gault*

The significance of *Gault* and its litany goes beyond a landmark decision in constitutional criminal procedure. The Court has rejected the contention that the promise to rehabilitate justifies waivering the youth's constitutional protections.

Subsequent Supreme Court decisions have expanded the rights of juveniles facing delinquency proceedings. In *In re Winship*, 397 U.S. 358, 90 S. Ct. 1068 (1969) the Court mandated the same burden of proof in juvenile delinquency proceedings as the one used in criminal prosecution, that is, proof beyond reasonable doubt. In *In re Breed v. Jones*, 421 U.S. 519, 95 S. Ct. 1779 (1975) it was established that trying youths in adult court for the same offense they were adjudicated for in juvenile court violated the double jeopardy clause of the Fifth Amendment. These youth could not be put twice at risk of losing their liberty and suffering stigmatization for the same offense. Citing *Gault*, the Supreme Court also noted that juvenile delinquency and adult criminal proceedings have similar consequences: "a proceeding where the issue is whether the child will be found to be 'delinquent' and subjected to the loss of his liberty for years is comparable in seriousness to a felony prosecution" (*In re Gault*, cited in Cohen, 1980: p. 601).

PARENS PATRIA DOCTRINE

Despite *Gault*, *Winship*, and *Breed*, the *parens patria* doctrine and the goal of rehabilitation remain the fundamental rationales of the juvenile justice system. The Court could not hold that criminal prosecution delivers punishment. Otherwise, it would have had no justification for denying juveniles all the constitutional protections accorded under such prosecutions (Kamisar, 1981: app. A, p. 20).[24]

CHILD'S DIMINISHED CAPACITY: A HISTORICAL PERSPECTIVE

The presumption of the minor's diminished capacity is, however, a recent social and legal invention rather than a fact of nature. Aries (1962) reported that in medieval times, children were treated as miniature adults. They mixed with adults and received no special consideration because of young age. During the Renaissance, the ideas of childhood and innocence held by Plato and Aristotle reappeared:

> The Hellenistic *paideia*, presupposed a difference and a transition between the world of children and that of adults, a transition made by means of an initiation or an education. Medieval civilization failed to perceive this difference and therefore lacked this concept of transition. The great event was therefore the revival, at the beginning of modern times, of an interest in education. (Aries, 1962: pp. 411–412)

Precursor of the Enlightenment, Locke describes children as minors who, lacking a certain amount of reason and understanding, can neither be as free as adults nor their equals. *"Children* I confess are not born in this full state of *Equality*, though they are born to it" (Locke, 1960: chap. 6, sec. 55). Children ought to be protected. Therefore, to grant them as much freedom as adults would be to harm them:

> To turn him loose to an unrestrain'd Liberty, before he has Reason to guide him, is not the allowing him the privilege of his Nature, to be free; but to thrust him out amongst Brutes, and abandon him to a state as wretched, and as much beneath that of a Man, as theirs. (Locke, 1960: chap. 6, sec. 63)

Rawls (1971) adopts a similar view: children have neither enough experience nor developed psychological and physical capabilities to decide autonomously. They deserve special treatment. At the constitutional convention stage, principles of paternalism are therefore chosen to protect children against their lack of reason and their incompetence.

PATERNALISTIC INTERVENTION: CONSENT

The delicate notion of consent underlies the concept of paternalistic intervention. Neither the disposition to agree nor the child's future "consent" is enough to legitimize such intervention. Through brainwashing and indoctrination parents could instill any belief or attitude in their children, who could no longer object once their autonomous thinking is permanently impaired. It would thus be cheating to call this future consent:

> Paternalistic principles are a protection against our own irrationality, and must not be interpreted to license assaults on one's convictions and character by any means so long as these offer the prospect of securing consent later on. More generally, methods of education must likewise honor these constraints. (Rawls, 1971: p. 250)

Under Rawls' theory, consent resulting from psychological brainwashing or lack of information cannot be justified. As children become more competent, parental interference should diminish. Parents should guide rather than substitute their opinions for those of their children. The basic principle in education would be that the only justified use of indoctrination is that use which will eventually make indoctrination ineffective by leading children to become their own centers of decision making.

AUTONOMOUS DECISION-MAKING ABILITY

A key term in this analysis is autonomous decision-making ability. Rather than assume a blanket diminished capacity from birth to eighteen years of age, Rawls perceives children as gradually developing their decision-making ability and as needing less and less parental interference.[25]

The idea of progressive exercise of liberty appears already in Locke's metaphor of "the swaddling clothes" that wrap the infant and progressively loosen:

> The Bonds of this Subjection are like the Swaddling Clothes they are wrapt up in, and supported by, in the weakness of their Infancy. Age and Reason as they grow up, loosen them till at length they drop quite off, and leave a Man at his own free Disposal. (Locke, 1960: chap. 6, sec. 55)

CONSTRAINTS ON *PARENS PATRIA* DOCTRINE

The individuals in the original position would therefore subject the *parens patria* doctrine to the constraints set by the principles of paternalism (Rawls, 1971). Parents and those acting in *loco parentis* would be allowed to decide for their children, provided:

1. That they choose for them as they would choose for themselves had they enjoyed adult capacities.

2. That they are guided by their children's wishes and preferences, as long as these are not irrational. It should be noted that the term irrational could be misused by parents, who may declare their children's preferences irrational because they do not correspond to their own. Thus, an interpretation of irrationality is needed, such as the one provided by Gewirth (1978), which is anything that could harm the child.

3. That if these wishes and preferences are unknown, they be guided by the criteria of primary goods.

Since at the constitutional convention stage children's talents, abilities, and preferences are not known, their will is replaced by an impersonal rational will. Rawls (1971) argues that "we try to get for him the things he [the child] presumably wants whatever else he wants" (p. 249). One helps children obtain wealth, opportunity, self-respect, and any other primary good that would stimulate the development of their capacity for autonomous choice.

Children are, therefore, not granted the same liberty rights as adults, but protection rights and rights based on need. Michaelman (1975) calls these rights welfare rights. Peffer (1978) names them social contract rights, and Gewirth (1978), preparatory rights. Whatever names given, these rights ask for children love, sympathy, intellectual and emotional stimulation, and any other psychological and social ingredients needed to develop the capacity to exercise their freedom. A bill in support of such rights has, in fact, been promulgated in the U.N. Declaration of the Rights of the Child (1960). (Some of its highlights may be found in appendix A of this book.)

CHILDREN'S RIGHT TO A SOCIAL MINIMUM

Because they are not risk takers, the Rawlsian individuals decide to protect their children's needs as rights at the constitutional level. They want to make sure that whatever their socioeconomic class, children will be provided with the resources and opportunities that will allow them to develop their freedom. This option is also chosen because it is easier to ascertain when basic rights are violated than it is to determine what socioeconomic policies are unjust. Rawls (1971) thus states:

> It is often perfectly plain and evident when the equal liberties are violated. These violations are not only unjust but can be clearly seen to be unjust: the injustice is manifest in the public structure of institutions. But this state of affairs is comparatively rare with social and economic policies regulated by the difference principle. (p. 199)

To be sure, welfare rights could not be provided in a society facing severely depressed economic conditions. But since the individuals of the original position know that their society has reached a certain level of well-being, they can claim these rights on behalf of their children.

Welfare rights could also be based on the principle of fair equality of opportunity, which must compensate for accidents of birth and fortune. Surely, fair equality of opportunity in education will be lacking as long as children lack food, love, and health:

> If so, the catalogue of insurance rights would reach beyond educational goods and (at least with regard to persons of educable age) into welfare domains which we tend to associate with the difference principle and the social minimum. And these additional rights seem more amenable to judicial definition than the core education claim itself, and more so under the opportunity principle than under the difference principle. (Michaelman, 1975: p. 344)

Finally, the right to a certain level of well-being may be derived from the most important primary good—self-respect. The satisfaction of children's basic needs is essential in order to prevent the psychological condition in which "persons lack a sure confidence in their own value and in their ability to do anything worthwhile" (Rawls, 1971: p. 535).

Thus, welfare rights are not linked uniquely to the difference principle, but also to the principle of liberty. Michaelman explains:

> Thus the difference principle implies welfare rights in the elusive form of whatever is necessary to prevent the undermining of self-respect by relative deprivation. The opportunity and liberty principles imply welfare rights as more objective, less relativistic biological entailments of opportunity and liberty. In addition, the central and preeminent good of self-respect may imply welfare rights reaching beyond those biological entailments, and not depending on notions of relative deprivation for their justification. (1975: p. 346)

ENFORCEMENT OF THE RIGHTS OF CHILDREN

Although children may have the right to grow up in an atmosphere of love and understanding, one may wonder how these claims could become enforceable legal entitlements. In the well-ordered society, the concept of right could be expanded to meet this objection. Quality of life claims would receive legal recognition and become moral grounds for reforming institutions affecting children. This idea is supported by Peffer's (1978) distinction between liberty rights and rights based on needs, which he calls social contract rights. Liberty rights entail the correlative obligation to respect those rights, and coercion of anyone who violates them.[26] In the case of social contract rights, there is no basis for such coercion. These rights arise from considering what ought to be done in a moral situation. They entail an obligation on the part of anyone who could do something about them, via the obligation to promote just institutions. However, if these obligations are not fulfilled, there are no grounds for coercion—but then society ceases to be just.

PATERNALISTIC AGENCIES

Although the individuals in the original position are presumed to adopt a child-centered view in their deliberations, it is not clear who is to assume the fulfillment of the obligations related to social contract rights. Should parents be granted absolute power over their children? To what extent should the state interfere? Would the individuals in the original position adopt the status quo or opt for alternative child-rearing practices?

In light of abuse, neglect, parental abdication of duties, and the potential threat of being subjected to incompetent and harmful parents, the individuals of the well-ordered society would want to protect children against those parents who transgress their natural duty of not harming the innocent (Rawls, 1971: p. 109), and against incompetent professionals paid to fend for abused and neglected children.

It is to be emphasized that throughout the history of Western society, parents' right to educate and nurture their children has never been an absolute right. This right has often been reassigned, attenuated, and sometimes relinquished. Parental powers, argues Locke, are connected to the obligation to nourish and educate their children. "So little power does the bare *act of begetting* give a Man over his Issue, if all his Care ends there, and this be all the Title he hath to the Name and Authority of a Father" (Locke, 1960: chap. 6, sec. 65). Aries (1962) reports that the practice of educating one's children is a recent phenomenon. Until the end of the eighteenth century, placing children in apprenticeship and delegating the responsibility of their education to a master was the norm at both ends of the social ladder. A master transmitted his art and knowledge to a child who was not his own.

In the well-ordered society, the right of paternalistic agency is, therefore, not automatically delegated to parents or to any other agents of society. It is conditional on how children's interests are best satisfied and protected.

THE LEAST-ADVANTAGED CHILDREN

Once the principles of paternalism and need-based rights have been formulated, the individuals of the original position move to the legislative stage. They have to promulgate laws and socioeconomic policies consistent with fair equality of opportunity and the difference principle.

The difference principle provides a criterion for ordering socioeconomic practices according to the benefits they bring to the least advantaged:

> In maximizing with respect to the least favored representative man, we need not go beyond ordinal judgments. If we can decide whether a change in the basic structure makes him better or worse off, we can determine his best situation. (Rawls, 1971: p. 92)

Rawls (1971), however, points out the difficulty of determining with accuracy whether socioeconomic institutions and practices regulated by the difference principle are just. Under nonideal conditions one is often reduced to choosing among several unjust arrangements. "Sometimes this scheme will include measures and policies that a perfectly just system would reject" (Rawls, 1971: p. 279).

The indices of primary goods, wealth, power, opportunity, and, most important self-respect, could allow for the location of least-advantaged children. In the nuclear family setting, these children may initially be found by determining their parents' socioeconomic status and standard of living.

The second index is that of social attitude. The support and encouragement parents give their children influence their life chances. And while many factors may affect this index, the disenfranchised and victims of economic and racial discrimination are disproportionately represented among the least advantaged.

The third index refers to whether children are given the opportunity to develop their inborn talents and abilities. Talents may be distributed throughout the various segments of the population, but children of low socioeconomic status have unequal chances to develop them. In his article "The Basic Structure as Subject," Rawls (1977) argues that although genetic components affect the development of one's abilities, environmental factors are pervasive:

> An ability is not, for example, a computer in the head with a definite measurable capacity unaffected by social circumstances. Among the elements affecting the realization of natural capacities are social attitudes of encouragement and support and the institutions concerned with their training and use . . . . So not only our final ends and hopes for ourselves but our realized abilities and talents reflect, to a large degree, our personal history, opportunities and social position. What we might have been had these things been different, we cannot know.   (p. 160)

It should be emphasized that the controversy of nature versus nurture is irrelevant to Rawls' theory of justice since the difference principle must compensate for undeserved inequalities, whether genetic or environmental.

The fourth and last index is self-respect. Children who are abused, neglected, and humiliated are most likely stripped of self-respect. They would be the best candidates for the position of the least advantaged.

Based on these four indices, a profile of the least advantaged can be drawn. They are youngsters of low socioeconomic status, children who rarely receive encouragement and support to develop their natural abilities and sense of self-worth. These children become the paramount challenge to the individuals of the well-ordered society during their deliberations about alternative child-rearing practices.

Chapter 3

Children's Fate in Western Society

In chapters 3 and 4, the nuclear and kibbutz families are placed within their respective socioeconomic contexts. The goal is to find out whether the inequalities tolerated by each of these ecological niches are compatible with the lexical ordering of the principles of justice, the difference principle, and the primary good of self-respect.

INEQUALITIES IN WESTERN SOCIETIES

Rawls (1971) acknowledges that the inequalities of wealth and power that exist in Western societies produce unequal liberties. Rich and poor may formally be equal before the law, but the rich enjoy better legal counsel. Rich and poor are entitled to participate equally in the political process, but the rich are more capable of securing laws that advance their interests. When applying this argument to institutions affecting children, Hirschi (1969), Schur (1973), and Thornberry (1973) found that at all levels of the juvenile justice system low-socioeconomic-status children are more severely treated than their middle-class counterparts:

> And it *is* true that the lower-class boy is more likely to be picked up by the police, more likely to be sent to juvenile court, more likely to be convicted, and more likely to be institutionalized if convicted, when he has committed the same crime as a middle-class boy. (Hirschi, 1969: p. 68)

Inequalities of wealth and power have cumulative effects. For instance, rich and poor may enjoy the same freedom of speech, but the rich have more access to and control over the mass media and are thus more free to make their views known and accepted. Low-income families living in disorganized neighborhoods and slums are also unable to pressure community and state institutions to be responsive to their children's needs. Poor mothers have reduced access to prenatal and other health care (Coopland, 1990). They are at greater risk of having premature births, children of low birth weight, and malnourished children (Garland, 1985). Furthermore, lower-class children with uneducated mothers suffer from cumulative IQ deficit. Intelligence Quotient differences between them and middle-class children, which are nonexistent in infancy, appear around three years of age and continue to increase (Broman, Nichols, & Kennedy, 1975; Farran, Haskins, & Gallagher, 1980; Golden & Birns, 1983).

LIBERTY VERSUS WORTH OF LIBERTY

Rawls (1971) tries to avoid addressing the problem of detrimental effects that inequalities of wealth and power produce on the exercise of liberty by introducing the concept worth of liberty. He argues that socioeconomic inequalities may cause inequality in the worth of liberty, but not inequality in liberty. Inequality in the worth of liberty is proportional to the capacity to advance one's ends and is regulated by the difference principle:

> The inability to take advantage of one's rights and opportunities as a result of poverty and ignorance, and a lack of means generally, is sometimes counted among the constraints definitive of liberty. I shall not, however, say this, but rather I shall think of these things as affecting the worth of liberty . . . . Freedom as equal liberty is equal for all . . . . But the worth of liberty is not the same for everyone. (Rawls, 1971: p. 204)

The distinction between liberty and worth of liberty is based on Rawls' definition of liberty, which states that one is free from this or that constraint to do so and so. Among those constraints are public opinion and social pressure, but economic factors are not mentioned (Rawls, 1971). It may be argued that the validity of Rawls' distinction depends on whether it is legitimate to exclude economic factors from the constraints defining liberty.

Economic factors seem just as constraining, since they create obstacles to the attainment of one's goals. For example, if parents want to send their children to a quality day-care center or to a private school but cannot afford to pay the tuition, they are no longer at liberty to do so. Furthermore, economic constraints are supported by laws that sometimes threaten the poor with the greatest possible loss of liberty: their lives. For instance, it is perfectly legal for a doctor or a hospital to refuse treatment to a patient who does not have money or insurance to pay the bills. Rawls (1971), however, argues that those with lesser worth of liberty are compensated for since their capacities would have been even more diminished had they not accepted the distribution regulated by the difference principle.

RELATIVE DEPRIVATION

Assuming the difference principle to have been satisfied and the quantity of primary goods of the least advantaged maximized, it may be argued that the worth of liberty of the least advantaged remains diminished, given their sensitivity to relative differences in the amount of primary goods obtained. The worth of liberty is affected by differential access to resources and institutions, such as legal counsel and mass media. As a result, the least advantaged end up in a relatively more disadvantaged position to exercise their liberty despite an increased index of primary goods.

SOCIOECONOMIC INEQUALITIES AND SELF-RESPECT

An additional argument related to self-respect undermines the distinction between liberty and the worth of liberty. For Rawls, the difference principle cannot regulate self-respect or the respect owed to others; otherwise, this primary good would depend on socioeconomic status. Because they have greater material possessions, people in higher socioeconomic strata would be more worthy of self-respect than those in lower ones. However, this position is unacceptable because people have the right to equal self-respect regardless of their socioeconomic status.

Equal citizenship liberties are, for Rawls, the sole valid basis of self-respect. Self-respect would then be equal because citizenship liberties are equal:

> The basis for self-esteem in a just society is not then one's income share but the publicly affirmed distribution of fundamental rights and liberties. And this distribution being equal, everyone has a similar, and secure status when they meet to conduct the common affairs of the wider society. (Rawls, 1971: p. 544)

One may, however, object that the public knowledge that the poor have unequal worth of liberty to exercise their basic rights and participate in the political process would be experienced by the poor as humiliating and therefore undermine their self-respect. Furthermore, if the individuals in the original position are not risk takers and grant liberty its priority, they would also realize that unequal worth of liberty is too risky. Great inequalities in wealth and power may raise the amount of primary goods of the least advantaged but simultaneously diminish their ability to exercise their rights and thus lower their self-esteem. To prevent this situation from occurring, the only rational option would be to choose equal worth of liberty for all.

INEQUALITIES AND MORAL DEVELOPMENT

A final argument reinforcing the choice of equal worth of liberty is that great disparities of wealth and power could stunt moral development. Rawls' model of moral development consists of three stages of morality: the morality of authority, the morality of association, and the morality of principles (Rawls, 1971). As one progresses through these stages one becomes more morally autonomous. Fisk (1975) argues that in a hierarchical socioeconomic structure such as ours, those in power would rarely reach the second stage of morality, which would allow them to cooperate and give equal status to the aspirations of those in the lower classes:

> The conflict stems from the greater or lesser remoteness from control over social production implied by the different roles. It is the conflict between landowner and peasant, union bureaucrat and the rank and file, welfare agent and the ghetto mother . . . . If indeed society has such a "class structure," then a sense of justice that involves taking a view of the whole will not be natural for humans as social beings. (Fisk, 1975: pp. 69–70)

To allow children to grow with self-respect and to develop a sense of justice, the individuals of the well-ordered society would opt for a more egalitarian socioeconomic system.

FREE-ENTERPRISE VERSUS SOCIALIST ECONOMIES

Whereas some may argue that in absolute terms capitalist societies produce more than socialist societies, several objections may be raised. Profit maximization often results in the exploitation of human and natural resources. If firing workers or investing overseas is more profitable, it is done without hesitation. The wealth of the capitalist would thus leak out to Thailand rather than trickle down to the South Bronx. Nevertheless, it may be that capitalist economies are more productive than socialist economies. It may be that the free market place unleashes innovative energies of individuals who develop new products and new markets. It may be that governmental bureaucracies of socialist economies squelch individuality and productivity. However, within a Rawlsian perspective, a fundamental flaw remains with capitalist economies:[27] even if in capitalist societies the least advantaged obtain a greater amount of primary goods in absolute terms than the average share in socialist societies, they continue to suffer from relative deprivation and consequent loss of self-respect.

RELATIVE DEPRIVATION AND SELF-RESPECT

Relative deprivation arises when people compare their low standard of living to that of the more affluent. Kornhauser (1978) argues that any value system that requires uniform socioeconomic criteria of success is imbalanced since it degrades those who fail to attain them by stripping them of self-respect. The effects of relative deprivation on self-respect are pervasive. Rawls (1971) seems to agree when he states that "the less fortunate are therefore often forcibly reminded of their situation, sometimes leading them to an even lower estimation of themselves and their mode of living" (p. 535).

Rawls (1971) also argues that capitalist calculation of the greatest sum of advantages and efficiency may lead to greater inequalities. Therefore, if fairness is to be achieved, these considerations cannot assume priority over the difference principle. In the well-ordered society, disparities of wealth and power are narrowed down in order to preserve the self-respect of the least advantaged:

> Although in theory the difference principle permits indefinitely large inequalities in return for small gains to the less favored, the spread of income and wealth should not be excessive in practice, given the requisite background institutions. (Rawls, 1971: p. 536)

> It follows that the confident sense of their own worth should be sought for the least favored and this limits the forms of hierarchy and the degree of inequalities that justice permits. (Rawls, 1971: p. 107)

RAWLS' PROGRAM OF SOCIOECONOMIC REFORMS

To minimize the inequalities allowed by the difference principle and to boost up the least advantaged, Rawls proposes a welfare economic program that would divide the government into four branches designed to regulate the initial distribution of income determined by competitive market economy. The function of the allocation branch would be to "keep the price system workably competitive and to prevent the formation of unreasonable market power" (Rawls, 1971: p. 276). The stabilization branch, second branch, would bring reasonably full employment "in the sense that those who want work can find it" (Rawls, 1971: p. 276). The transfer branch, third branch, would determine the social minimum based on need and the standard of living that should be guaranteed to all. To achieve this goal, Rawls (1971) argues for a graded income supplement rather than a minimum wage because competitive markets are ill-suited to answer claims of need. Furthermore, minimum wage may interfere with free enterprise. The distribution branch, fourth branch of the government, has two functions. The first is to impose taxes on inheritance, gifts, and the right of bequest in order to prevent the concentration of wealth and power. The second is to establish negative income tax that will provide the resources for the realization of the principle of fair equality of opportunity and the difference principle in education and in other social contexts. To eliminate poverty, adjustments would be made to intensify tax transfer activity. Graduated negative income and property taxes would reduce the gap between top and bottom income levels.

HIGH SOCIAL MINIMUM

Because of heavy taxation of the rich and transfer of money to the poor one would expect the least advantaged to have reached a high social minimum. But Rawls tries to avoid this consequence:

> Now offhand it might seem that the difference principle requires a very high social minimum. One naturally imagines that the greater wealth of those better off is to be scaled down until eventually everyone has nearly the same income. But this is a misconception, although it might hold in special circumstances. (1971: p. 285)

He argues that, in fact, the social minimum should not be "too high" because excessive governmental taxation would prevent economic expansion and have the opposite consequence to that expected, namely, that of lowering the standard of living of all—including that of the least advantaged. This is so, in part, because under governmental interference, the most advantaged would be reluctant to invest and thereby expand the economy by creating additional jobs and services. Rawls (1971) refers the reader to the law of supply and demand and to other aspects of the free market place to support his position. He also argues that excessive taxation would prevent parents from saving for their children and in turn prevent the next generation from maintaining just institutions. Thus, heavy taxation leading to a high social minimum should be rejected. The point for determining the appropriate social minimum is that point beyond which:

> Either the appropriate savings cannot be made or the greater taxes interfere so much with economic efficiency that the prospects of the least advantaged in the present generation are no longer improved but begin to decline. In either event the correct minimum has been reached. (Rawls, 1971: p. 286)

RAWLS' SOCIOECONOMIC PROGRAM CRITICIZED

Rawls' program of socioeconomic reform and the weak application of the difference principle could hardly achieve the well-ordered society. By providing the poor with an income supplement rather than equal or minimum wage, the transfer branch distributes stigma as well as money. A nonemployed food stamp recipient who buys steak would have less self-respect than a customer who is employed but can only afford hot dogs. The latter may value himself as a hard worker, while the former ends up feeling like a worthless parasite. Income supplements, which stigmatize and degrade the poor, are incompatible with the notion of equal respect owed to all.

EQUAL OPPORTUNITY FOR CHILDREN

One may wonder what the implications of Rawls' program for children are and whether it allows for the application of the principle of fair equality of opportunity. Nozick (1974) argues that it is unfortunate, but neither unjust nor unfair, that equality of opportunity does not obtain in our society. To the contrary, for Rawls, a socioeconomic system in which children's prospects are determined by their parents' productivity and inherited wealth is unjust. Negative income tax, inheritance taxation, and just savings should provide funding for children's education. "The government tries to insure equal chances of education and culture for persons similarly endowed and motivated either by subsidizing private schools or by establishing a public school system" (Rawls, 1971: p. 275).

In summary, Rawls' socioeconomic program may improve the situation of the poor and reduce some of the incidents of child abuse, neglect, and instability that result from poverty, but it would not prevent the consequences that social stigma and relative deprivation have on self-respect.

THE NUCLEAR FAMILY: BARRIER TO FAIR EQUALITY OF OPPORTUNITY

Rawls (1971) discusses the ramifications of the existence of the nuclear family as an economic unit. In the quotation given in this section, it seems to Rawls that fair equality of opportunity within the context of the nuclear family will never be achieved. He realizes that a deeper meaning of fair equality of opportunity requires not only an improvement in socioeconomic status, but a happy family life, attitudes of encouragement and support, and a certain quality of parenting. These factors imply a society in which not only material but psychological and intellectual resources are made available to all children alike. However, the family may be a barrier to such equality:

We should however note that although the internal life and culture of the family influence, perhaps as much as anything else, a child's motivation and his capacity to gain from education, and so in turn his life prospects, these effects are not necessarily inconsistent with fair equality of opportunity. Even in a well-ordered society that satisfies the two principles of justice, the family may be a barrier to equal chances between individuals. For as I have defined, the second principle only requires equal life prospects in all sectors of society for those similarly endowed and motivated. If there are variations among families in the same sector in how they shape the child's aspirations, then while fair equality of opportunity may obtain between sectors, equal chances between individuals will not. (Rawls, 1971: p. 301)

Rawls (1971) raises the question of abolishing the family in order to effectuate fair equality of opportunity, but he does not answer it:

The consistent application of the principle of fair opportunity requires us to view persons independently from the influences of their social position. But how far should this tendency be carried? It seems that even when fair opportunity (as it has been defined) is satisfied, the family will lead to unequal chances between individuals. Is the family to be abolished then? Taken by itself and given a certain primacy, the idea of fair equality of opportunity inclines in this direction. (Rawls, 1971: p. 511)

For the same reasons, Charvet (1969) argues that many socioeconomic structures, and especially the family, prevent the realization of equality of opportunity:

If one starts by considering the opportunity to attain superior positions in adult practices, one is rapidly led backward into arguing that the opportunity to obtain the education that will enable one to claim superior positions should be equal for all. But one can't stop at schools, for the development of one's abilities doesn't begin there, but in the family, where being brought up by certain parents will give one an initial start over one's contemporaries less favoured in their parents. (p. 4)

To achieve equality of opportunity, all factors affecting success, such as effective parents, teachers, and schools, should be controlled and evenly distributed among children. But this endeavor is impossible short of cloning through genetic and environmental engineering (Charvet, 1969).

One may object, as Nielsen (1985) does, that even though equality of opportunity cannot be realized absolutely, different conditions may in varying degrees approach its realization. One could, for example, fight legal and de facto barriers based on sex, race, and socioeconomic background.

Mass media could concentrate on reducing sociopolitical indifference. Teachers could attempt to have more input into ameliorating schooling deficiencies resulting from impoverished family background. If all these things obtained, one would move closer to achieving equality of opportunity.

Nevertheless, differences in family background would still remain as crucial impediments to equality of opportunity. Even if the quality of teachers is the same, children of impoverished background do not perform as well in school as do children coming from more privileged families. Families in poverty are rarely able to provide a supportive and stimulating environment to foster the development of their children. Parents in poverty and of limited education talk less to their children, provide them with fewer toys, spend less time stimulating them, and more often administer physical punishment to their children than do middle-class parents (Farran, Haskins, & Gallagher, 1980). Children living in families below the poverty line are nearly twice as likely to be retained in class than are children in nonpoverty families (Bianchi, 1984), and children from lowest-income families are twice as likely to drop out of school (Stedman, Salganik, & Celebuski, 1988).

Nielsen (1985), therefore, proposes to abolish the family and to increase the number of state nurseries and boarding schools.[28] He concludes that there may be practical and moral objections against this proposal, but no conceptual arguments could stand against it.

Some may want to object that even though the least advantaged are deprived, the more advantaged children would be better off within a nuclear family setting. This contention is, however, irrelevant to the advocates of justice as fairness, since the criterion for any socioeconomic reform remains the improvement of the prospects of the least advantaged.

Chapter 4

The Kibbutz Egalitarian Society

NATURAL ENDOWMENT AS A COMMON ASSET

The individuals in the original position choose the principle of fair equality of opportunity rather than the principle of liberal equality of opportunity because although the latter may provide an equal start to those with similar talents and abilities regardless of their socioeconomic status, it is still influenced by natural abilities such as talents and intelligence. For them, any distribution of primary goods determined by talents and abilities is morally arbitrary, like any distribution based on wealth and inheritance. In the well-ordered society, everyone undertakes to consider natural endowments as common assets and to share the benefits that flow from them with the less fortunate. "Those who have been favored, by nature, whoever they are, may gain from their good fortune only on terms that improve the situation of those who have lost out" (Rawls, 1971: p. 101).

The reason for considering talents and abilities common assets is that their development and value depend on social cooperation and social institutions. The more talented members of the well-ordered society acknowledge that other people have contributed to the development of their talents and abilities and are willing to share the rewards their talents bring:

> The naturally advantaged are not to gain merely because they are more gifted, but only to cover the costs of training and education and for using their endowments in ways that help the less fortunate as well. No one deserves his greater natural capacity nor merits a more favorable starting place in society. But it does not follow that one should eliminate these distinctions . . . . The basic structure can be arranged so that these contingencies work for the good of the least fortunate. (Rawls, 1971: pp. 101–102)

DESERT AND NATURAL ABILITIES

Rawls (1971) rejects any notion of desert related to natural abilities: "No one deserves his place in the distribution of native endowments, any more than one deserves one's initial starting place in society" (p. 104). One is only entitled to have legitimate expectations, but these have no meaning prior to the establishment of social institutions.

As noted in chapter 2, the debate over what determines intelligence, nature or nurture, loses its importance for Rawls because of its lack of moral relevance. Furthermore, once talents and natural abilities are considered common assets, it does not really matter who possesses them and why.

THE WELL-ORDERED SOCIETY: A SOCIAL UNION

By accepting the difference principle, the most advantaged seem to gain much less than what they would otherwise have, had they derived advantages from their abilities. Adherence to this principle thus reflects a developed sense of justice as well as a profound sense of community grounded on the ideals of sharing and fraternity. Rawls states that

> the difference principle expresses a conception of reciprocity. It is a principle of mutual benefit . . . . The difference principle corresponds to the natural meaning of fraternity: namely the idea of not wanting to have greater advantages unless this is to benefit others who are less well-off. (Rawls, 1971: p. 102, p. 130)

The individuals of the well-ordered society participate in a social union and value their cooperation as a good in itself (Rawls, 1971). Their sense of community is manifested in their motivation, values, and fraternal feelings. Their community supports their self-esteem and provides an additional basis for self-respect. Rawls reminds us that a sense of community does not emerge in the more talented only, but in all members of the well-ordered society. No matter how individualistic a conception of justice is, one must "explain the value of community. Otherwise the theory of justice cannot succeed" (Rawls, 1971: p. 265).

KIBBUTZ PIONEERS AND THE ORIGINAL POSITION

Kibbutz pioneers created a socioeconomic structure implementing ideals similar to Rawls', such as sharing, mutual help, and social union. One could easily imagine them bargaining about the principles of justice that were to underlie their society. Strict equality in all spheres of life was initially chosen, namely, equal liberty, equality of opportunity, and equal distribution in other primary goods. Indeed, by attempting a fair distribution of socioeconomic goods other than liberty, kibbutzniks' conception of justice culminated in the implementation of a principle similar to the difference principle.

The kibbutz is based on the ideal of the Jewish farmer laboring on collectively owned land. In this society there are no employers or employees. Political and economic decisions are made by members themselves. Goods are distributed according to the Marxist dictum "from each according to his ability to each according to his needs."

Middle-class intellectuals, the pioneers perceived asceticism as a precondition to the realization of the ideals of national renaissance, Zionism, and socialism. National renaissance depended on the ability to save, invest, and create a self-supporting economy. The goal was to establish socialist cells throughout Israel and to exercise political influence through personal example and participation. By adopting a simple way of living, the pioneers were showing their solidarity with the working class throughout the world. Material rewards had little meaning to them and were not primary incentives (Ben-Yosef, 1963; Leon, 1969).

PRESENT-DAY KIBBUTZIM

The declaration of independence of Israel and the establishment of statehood in 1948 marked a turning point from asceticism to a more consumer oriented ideology. The kibbutz lost its central role in Israel's political and social life. Revolutionary ideals no longer evoked the individual's full-time commitment. Consolidation of the economy created a division of labor that increased group heterogeneity.

After reaching a point of diminishing returns, kibbutzim could no longer be solely agricultural. They began to develop small and medium-sized industrial shops enmeshed within their social structure. However, industrialization in the sociological sense has not occurred (Golomb, 1980; Tannenbaum, 1980). There has been no dislocation of population, urbanization, and bureaucratization. Despite the diversification of the economy, kibbutz members remain committed to communal child-rearing ideology and socialist ideals. However, they are no longer indifferent to the quantity of goods they can receive from social cooperation. They ask the kibbutz to keep its socialist promise of being able to provide workers with better conditions than those of other workers in "capitalist" Israel (Talmon-Garber, 1972).

Increased consumerism has multiplied individual taste and made it impossible to distribute the same goods to everyone. Kibbutzim now adopt the practice of personal budgeting for clothing, vacations, and other personal expenditures. Each family is allowed its share of per capita expenditure.

APPLICATION OF THE PRINCIPLE OF EQUAL LIBERTY

Kibbutz members have the same liberty rights as other Israeli citizens, such as freedom of speech and equal participation in political affairs. Kibbutz membership is voluntary. After a probationary period, candidates who identify with the kibbutz ideals of mutual help and social cooperation may apply for membership. The general assembly, in which every kibbutznik is a member, must approve the request by a majority vote. This sovereign body has unlimited authority. About 40 percent of the kibbutz members participate in its weekly meetings, during which socioeconomic, political, and cultural policies are discussed, committees created, and economic plans ratified. Typical topics of discussion may relate to increasing the personal budget, reorganization of an agricultural branch, or the creation of an industrial shop.

With the expansion of the economy and the need for professional expertise, the general assembly has delegated more and more of its authority to the secretariat[29] and to numerous committees, which are responsible for the organization of various aspects of kibbutz life such as education, festivals, and other communal activities.

Individually autonomous kibbutzim join into major federations.[30] Each federation sponsors joint enterprises in research, educational and training programs, and advisory services. It provides loans and dispatches experienced kibbutzniks to assist kibbutzim in need. Nowhere is the difference principle and the norm of mutual aid more clearly applied than in the federation's decision to help its least advantaged kibbutzim. Whereas private businesses would eliminate nonprofitable units, the kibbutz federation does not allow for the dissolution of disadvantaged kibbutzim and provides for its members' needs on a year-round basis regardless of seasonal labor requirements or workers' productivity. These policies may lower the earnings of more affluent kibbutzim, but in this socioeconomic structure, fairness precedes profit maximization.

APPLICATION OF THE PRINCIPLE OF FAIR EQUALITY OF OPPORTUNITY

Applying the principle of fair equality of opportunity, the kibbutz prevents centralization of power and the rise of bureaucracy. Members responsible for the overall administration of the kibbutz such as the secretary of the kibbutz, treasurer, work allocator, and managers of production and consumption branches seem most advantaged by the criteria of power and authority.

However, frequent election of these officeholders and their rotation every one to three years provide the opportunity to anyone with requisite skills to participate in the exercise of power. Approximately 50 percent of the kibbutz members at any given time serve on one or more of the various committees. With the increase of candidates for public office, more and more members are, therefore, capable of assuming various positions of authority, and consolidation of powerful groups is thus prevented. Furthermore, rewards and privileges derived from high-status positions requiring special talent and ability are minimal. This consequence would also be entailed by Rawls' system of justice, within which fair equality of opportunity in education and in the job market would increase the number of qualified individuals and reduce the rewards these qualifications bring.

In this structure, the precept "from each according to his contribution" in the sense of each according to his education and training assumes less importance than the precept "from each according to his effort." The individuals in the well-ordered society would also adopt effort rather than productivity or achievement as a criteria of evaluation (Rawls, 1971).

DISTRIBUTION OF INCOME, POWER, AND SELF-RESPECT

Kibbutz officeholders thus obtain few material rewards. They may have more opportunity to travel, better access to communal institutions, and a slightly larger share of personal allowance, but these advantages are not status symbols. They are also granted to students residing outside the kibbutz or to the drivers of officeholders. If the latter must spend the night in a hotel in town with their "boss," they will enjoy the same type of meal and the same type of room. Furthermore, officeholders may have more power in the sphere of their expertise, but they cannot abuse their power for personal ends. If their directions are not followed or if they cannot obtain cooperation, they cannot apply sanctions directly. They must bring the problem to the general assembly or one of its committees.

The balance of rewards and tensions connected to the various kibbutz management appointments was found to vary according to the various positions held (Talmon-Garber, 1972). The managers of the various branches in industry and agriculture obtain most of the rewards and experience least tension. Their expertise is generally unquestioned. To the contrary, the managers of the consumption branch enjoy fewer positive rewards and face greater tension. They are constantly criticized by other kibbutzniks who consider themselves as competent as they are in this domain. Finally, the members of the secretariat experience the greatest tension. Being responsible for the coordination and smooth functioning of various branches, they must accommodate other members' pressing demands. Thus in the kibbutz, as it would conceivably be in the well-ordered society, those who enjoy the most power gain only limited rewards. "The relative difference in earnings between the more favored and the lowest income class tends to close; and this tendency is even stronger when the difference principle is followed" (Rawls, 1971: p. 307).

Renumeration: Wages versus Yearly Allowance

Although the principle of fair equality of opportunity is chosen on the grounds that the distribution of socioeconomic primary goods should not be determined by differences in talents or abilities, Rawls makes no attempt to change the initial distribution of rewards caused by these differences. His (1971) taxation program is supposed to remove only the worst aspect of so-called wage slavery. According to him, this is the best one could hope to achieve. Rawls (1971) also contends that controlling the market by a socialist economy is no more just than the control exercised by means of market prices. In practice, one is faced with the dilemma of choosing between several unjust arrangements.

Assuming the well-ordered society was achieved, its members would be faced with the options of wages or a system of renumeration similar to that existing in the kibbutz. Since in the well-ordered society talents and abilities are considered common assets and the rewards derived from them are not tied to social position, it seems reasonable to consider these rewards to be held in common. Its members would thus receive, as in the kibbutz, a yearly per capita allowance instead of a salary.

SOCIAL SOLIDARITY

Although kibbutz members receive no wages, they are highly motivated and productive. As a result, kibbutzniks account for up to 25 percent of the nation's political leaders (Katz, 1980: p. 198) and excel in the nation's military (Amir, 1969). Whereas they comprise only 3.6 percent of Israel's Jewish population, they produce up to 50 percent of the country's agricultural production and 9 percent of its industrial production (Kantor, 1988: p. 16).

A unique characteristic of the kibbutz socioeconomic structure is its social solidarity. Kibbutz members have a strong esprit de corps that is not lowered by differences in salary or income supplement. They enjoy psychological and material security. They do not have to face problems of seasonal or cyclical unemployment. If they are sick or disabled, their standard of living will not change. Above all else, kibbutz members are free from economic competitiveness and from the anxiety and isolation arising from it. They know that their standard of living will rise only if everyone contributes to the group's efforts. In Rawlsian terms, they understand that if they want to be better off, they must first improve the situation of those who are worse off, and that members' expectations are interwoven into a "close knit." They cannot alter the expectations of any particular kibbutz member without at the same time affecting the expectations of every other kibbutz member.

Kibbutzniks' self-respect and sense of worth do not depend on the arbitrary socioeconomic hierarchies of capitalist societies or on the privileges dispensed by bureaucracies in a communist bloc. This system minimizes the sources of envy arising from differences of status and power that make social cooperation impossible (Rawls, 1971). Rosner (1970) expresses kibbutzniks' feelings of belongingness and of sharing the same fate:

> In the kibbutz the emotional attachment of the individual kibbutz member to his peer group and to the kibbutz as a whole almost eliminated the feeling of isolation, of loneliness in the crowd, of anomie, so familiar to modern mass society. The membership in this group creates a feeling of belonging, of sharing the fate of others, which are the conditions for real synergy and cooperation between human beings. (p. 89)

The kibbutz implements the ideals of mutual aid and community. Like the individuals in the original position, kibbutz members reject any conception of society in which social cooperation is perceived as a necessary burden to achieve one's ends. Social cooperation is for them an end in itself—a social union of individuals. "We need one another as partners in ways of life that are engaged in for their own sake, and the successes and enjoyments of others are necessary for and complimentary to our own good" (Rawls, 1971: pp. 522–523).

Kibbutzniks participate in many social unions by working in groups and various committees. Each sector of the kibbutz economy is divided into branches and work is done in teams. Whereas the principle of work equality does not eliminate differences in abilities, it suppresses arbitrary hierarchical distinctions. Managers put their expertise to the service of others. There is no employer and no employee, and no separate managerial or bureaucratic class. Participation in decisionmaking of all workers within semi-autonomous groups composed of six to nine members and rotation of supervisory positions are kibbutz norms. This type of division of labor allows for greater communal solidarity.[31]

Rawls argues that only within such a type of community could one self-actualize—not by each becoming complete in himself, but by meaningful work within a just social union. Individuals' potentialities far exceed what they could hope to realize in a lifetime. By participating in many social unions, individuals with similar or complementary talents could cooperate to overcome partiality and finitude and realize their common nature (Rawls, 1971).

The intellectual level and interest of kibbutz members are high. Every settlement has its choir, orchestra, drama, folk music, and dancing as well as group discussions. Sartre, who visited one of the kibbutzim and apparently never changed his view, commented:

> On kibbutz I found the realisation of the vision which Marx once expressed—that the day would come when the difference between the man who labours with his hands and the intellectuals would disappear. We saw in the kibbutz farmers who are at one and the same time the intellectuals and workers. They are shepherds and are informed in literature, sociology and politics. This isn't so simple and there exists a dialectical contradiction in this area, but we found here a uniqueness in unity. (J. P. Sartre, cited in Leon, 1969: pp. 41–42)

EQUAL OPPORTUNITY FOR WOMEN

In Israel's pioneer days women worked in the field side by side with men, but with the increase in the number of children and the rise in standard of living, or simply because of personal preference and affinity, many women choose careers in education and services. Nevertheless, women are still overrepresented in dull, monotonous jobs. The kibbutz tries to maintain its egalitarian ideology by providing jobs for both sexes in social work, psychology, counseling, and the arts. It also seeks to achieve proportional representation of women on committees. Because of its social norms, the kibbutz solicits nominated women to accept positions, which enable them to gain experience and actively participate.

Engels (1942) argued that class oppression underlies formal equality between capitalist and proletarian. Similarly, formal equality between sexes reveals the oppression of women and the changes necessary to liberate them. If women could fully participate in the labor force, private property and the family as a separate economic and child-rearing unit would be abolished. With the transfer of the means of production into common ownership, the nuclear family would cease to be the building block of the economy. Care and education of children would become public enterprise. Society would take care of all children alike.

Freeing women from their traditional roles and removing the barriers that prevented them from playing an equal role, the kibbutz apparently applied Engels' program. In the kibbutz women do not feel guilty because they are at work while their children are in nurseries. Communal education allows them to fully participate in all aspects of communal life.

FAIR EQUALITY OF OPPORTUNITY FOR CHILDREN

Assuming once more that the well-ordered society has been achieved, it may be assumed that the application of the difference principle has narrowed down socioeconomic differences in family background. However, differences in quality of parenting and attitudes of encouragement and support, which are so crucial to the child's development and success, still remain because of the existence of the nuclear family. Rawls (1971) holds that it seems to be the case, and Nielsen (1985) holds that it is the case that the nuclear family is a barrier to fair equality of opportunity.

Plato (1965) also recommended abolishing the nuclear family, which had to become communal rather than nuclear. The community of people and property would prevent the city from being torn between what is mine and what is yours: all would work toward common goals.

The kibbutz is arguably a variation of Rawls', Nielsen's, and Plato's ideas, and it improves upon their conception. The kibbutz family does not exist as an economic unit. And although children no longer sleep at the children's house but at their parents' home, they spend the greater part of their waking hours in various kibbutz educational institutions. The kibbutz as a whole is a *michpacha*, that is, a family. Children are the children of the community, which functions as a large extended family. Highly productive members, among whom childless couples and bachelors are included, do not feel unfairly treated because they have to contribute to the support and education of all the children of their community.

Regardless of whether they are the children of unskilled workers or of doctors, and even if they do not have any parents in the kibbutz, children's share in socioeconomic and cultural goods is according to need. It has also been an integral kibbutz enterprise to raise and educate orphans and underprivileged city children. The Youth Aliyah/Chevrot Noar program has been responsible for the immigration and absorption of over 200,000 Jewish children from all over the world (Horn, 1984: p. 14). Initiated in 1933 in order to save the children from Hitler's Europe, this project became an avenue for helping thousands of Sepharadic refugee children from Arab countries.[32] Presently, it reaches out to children of immigrants from Ethiopia, from the former Soviet Union and Yugoslavia, and from other oppressive countries. Underprivileged, poverty-stricken, or disintegrated families also have the opportunity to entrust their 13- to 18-year-old children to the kibbutz, which provides them an education they could not otherwise afford. The Chevrot Noar project accounts for approximately one-fourth of kibbutz high school enrollment (Near, 1982).

In conclusion, communal education eliminates socioeconomic, psychological, and cultural inequalities in child rearing and thus realizes a higher form of the ideal of fair equality of opportunity. It satisfies the difference principle by making available to all its children not only its socioeconomic but also its cultural and psychological resources.

Chapter 5

Social Conformity and Deviance: Kibbutz versus Nuclear-Family Children

Parents are imagined returning to the original position in order to choose the child-rearing institutions that would stimulate the intellectual and moral development of their children. One of the criteria used during their deliberations is the improvement of the prospects of juvenile delinquents, who have often been abused, neglected, and stripped of the most important primary good—self-respect. The child-rearing structure, nuclear or kibbutz family, that would prevent or at least minimize abuse, neglect, and delinquency, and allow for the development of strong social bonds and autonomous moral behavior, is expected to be chosen.

RESEARCH METHODOLOGY

Research was conducted in Israel in 1986 in order to validate theoretical arguments about the relative strength of the social bonds of kibbutz and nuclear-family children. Self-report appeared to be the only legitimate instrument because in the kibbutz there are no police or other formal agents of social control. Furthermore, in this society delinquent acts are rarely reported to outside authorities; consequently, there are no reliable official data concerning delinquency in the kibbutz. Our target population—the kibbutz and nuclear-family children—was composed of white high school students[33] for whom the superiority of self-report had been established (see appendix B).

Hirschi (1969), a proponent of self-report, analyzes deviance and conformity in terms of social bonds operationally defined as consisting of (1) attachment, the emotional component; (2) commitment, the rational component; and (3) belief, the normative component. These three components correspond to Rawls' three stages of morality: the morality of authority, the morality of association, and the morality of principles. Each stage depends for its development on the attainment of the previous one and represents a more mature sense of justice.

These and many other similarities between Hirschi's and Rawls' theories make Hirschi's operationalization of various moral concepts relevant to Rawls'. Hirschi's self-report questionnaire was adopted as our research tool (see appendix C).[34] It was translated into Hebrew and administered to 24 kibbutz and 24 nuclear-family children 13 to 17 years of age, chosen randomly.[35] A chi-square statistic at $p < .05$ was used to determine the significance of the differences between kibbutz and nuclear-family data.

ATTACHMENT AND MORALITY OF AUTHORITY

For Rawls and Hirschi, children are born amoral and self-interested. Moved by instincts, they do not have any conception of right or wrong. Society, through its various institutions—the family, the school, and the law—teaches children normative behavior. Quoting Hobbes, Hirschi (1969) explains that man's passions and actions are in themselves no sin until they know a law that forbids them. Man's nature becomes human nature only after socialization, moralization, and training. Compared to man's desires, social limitations are weak. Individuals are aware that conventional means are scarce and that through nonnormative routes needs are gratified easier and faster. They are always sufficiently motivated to deviate. Thus, Hirschi argues that conformity rather than deviance needs to be explained. His answer to the question, "Why doesn't everybody commit delinquent acts?" fits the social control model of delinquency: strong controls and social bonds prevent individuals from giving in to temptation and deviating.

Attachment is the emotional component of the social bond. It is expressed by love and respect, which are fundamental to the acquisition of morality. Hirschi (1969) found a direct link between attachment to one's parents and the strength of one's beliefs in the moral validity of social norms: "The emotional bond between the parent and the child presumably provides the bridge across which pass parental ideas and expectations" (p. 86). Rawls (1971) equally argues that children, who are at first totally self-interested, comply with their parents' prohibitions and follow their precepts only if they feel loved, cared for, and respected. Hirschi (1969) quotes Piaget to stress the same point:

> It is not the obligatory character of the rule laid down by an individual that makes us respect this individual, it is the respect we feel for the individual that makes us regard as obligatory the rule he lays down. The

appearance of the sense of duty in a child thus admits of the simplest explanation, namely that he receives commands from older children (in play) and from adults (in life), and that he respects older children and parents. (Piaget, cited in Hirschi, 1969: pp. 29–30)

Youths growing up in poor neighborhoods who are attached to their parents and perceive their mothers as affectionate are less likely to commit delinquent acts, regardless of their poverty level (Glueck & Glueck, 1972; McCord, McCord, & Zola, 1959).

Conversely, parents who are indifferent and neglectful and adopt erratic discipline alienate their children and no longer can teach them to respect the social norms (Hirschi, 1969; Moore, Pauker, & Moore, 1984). Rawls (1971) points out that "in the absence of affection, example, and guidance, none of these processes can take place, and certainly not in loveless relationships maintained by coercive threats and reprisals" (p. 466). Children who are not attached to their parents have little stake in conformity. They feel free to violate parental injunctions, which are no longer, or never were, important to them.

Hirschi (1978) argues that future attachments could hardly compensate for lack of attachment to one's parents. Children with a long history of parental abuse and neglect have lost the capacity to belong. This position reflects the psychoanalytic orientation of Bowlby (1965), Harlow and Harlow (1969), and Spitz (1946), who maintained that attachment to and a continuous relationship with the mother constitute the basis for a healthy personality:

On the basis of this varied evidence it appears that there is a very strong case indeed for believing that prolonged separation of a child from his mother (or mother-substitute) during the first five years of life stands foremost among the causes of delinquent character development and persistent misbehavior. (Bowlby, cited in Hirschi, 1969: p. 86)

Attachment and Kibbutz Child-Rearing Patterns

The fundamental components of kibbutz child-rearing structure are its multiple caretakers, the prominence of the peer group as a socializing agent, and the attachment of children to many adults. Kibbutz parents are not the primary socializing agents. Traditionally, kibbutz children from birth lived at the children's house and only saw their parents a couple of hours every afternoon, on weekends, and on holidays. The kibbutz youth examined in this research were raised in this manner. However, to meet the demand for familism, kibbutzim have changed children's sleeping arrangements. Up to 13 years of age, children now sleep in their parents' apartment (Kibbutz Conference, 1992). From 13 through 18 years of age, kibbutz adolescents continue to live away from their parents in the Youth Society's quarters. The Youth Society, which is semi-autonomous and modeled after the adult society, is discussed in chapter 6.

Infants and children spend the greatest part of their day, from 7 A.M. to 3 P.M., away from their parents under the care of the *metapelet*. She is an educator, nurse, and maid who schedules the children's daily routine: what they eat, how they dress, and what they do. The *metapelet* is usually very task oriented. Relieving the discomfort of many children, she cannot be monopolized by any one of them. Children have to learn to share her. This fact is often an impetus for autonomous behavior, since the children's only alternative to waiting indefinitely for her help is to alleviate frustration by themselves.

It may be argued that the care the *metapelet* provides cannot compensate for children's "prolonged" separation from their mothers. Kibbutz children may thus be expected to experience maternal deprivation and neglect. Indeed, Bowlby (1965) and Yarrow (1961), after conducting research in the kibbutz and finding a higher rate of bed-wetting, thumbsucking, and temper tantrums than in the nuclear-family control group, concluded that these symptoms must be signs of personality disturbance. Further research, however, indicated that these phenomena rather reflect cultural differences in upbringing. Kibbutzniks are more permissive and do not punish children for such behaviors. Eisenberg (1965) found kibbutz children to grow into mature and capable individuals, and Rabin (1965), who compared kibbutz to nuclear-family children ($\underline{N} = 38$) on Rorschach tests, found them to be more accurate in their perception of reality and to exhibit greater maturity.

Identification and Communication

Since by comparison to nuclear-family children, kibbutz children spend less time with their parents, they may be expected to communicate less with their parents and to perceive them as less affectionate or supportive. On the basis of these criteria, kibbutz children may be expected to be less attached to their parents than nuclear-family children are to their parents. Hirschi's operationalization of attachment into identification, communication, rejection, and support allows for empirical testing of this hypothesis.

Percentage comparisons between nuclear family and kibbutz youths on the indices of identification, communication, and feelings of rejection and support with their mothers, fathers, and friends are presented in tables 5.1 through 5.4. These tables combine a set of questions kibbutz and nuclear-family children were asked about their mothers, fathers, and friends. For instance, to assess the identification of the nuclear-family and kibbutz children with their mothers, fathers, and friends, the following questions were asked: "Would you like to be the kind of person your father is?", "Would you like to be the kind of person your mother is?", and "Would you like to be the kind of person your friends are?" These three questions were condensed in table 5.1 under the title "Would you like to be the kind of person these people are?" Tables 5.2 through 5.4 follow the same pattern.

Fewer kibbutz than nuclear-family children were found to identify with their parents (table 5.1), but slightly more kibbutz children were found to share feelings and thoughts with their parents (table 5.2). However, these differences were too small to be significant ($p > .05$). Nonetheless, significantly more kibbutz than nuclear-family children were found to communicate with their parents and to perceive communication as going in both directions between them and their parents. Similarly, significantly more kibbutz than nuclear-family children ($p < .05$) were able to talk to their fathers about future plans (table 5.3), and to perceive their parents as helping when they encountered things they did not understand (table 5.4).[36] Hirschi (1969) explains that the degree of identification with parents (table 5.1) is not significantly related to one's attachment to them: what counts is the degree of communication with parents. Whatever the degree of children's identification with their parents, as the intimacy of communication increases, the strength of their attachment to their parents increases and the likelihood of deviance decreases.

Table 5.1

Percentage of Youth Answering to the Question
"Would you like to be the kind of person these people are?"

	Kibbutz			Nuclear Family		
	Fathers	Mothers	Friends[a]	Fathers	Mothers	Friends[a]
Most/Some Ways	62.5	37.5	54.2	70.8	50	91.7
Not At All	37.5	62.5	45.8	29.2	50	8.3
	100	100	100	100	100	100
	(24)	(24)	(24)	(24)	(24)	(24)

a. χ^2 (1, $N = 48$) = 8.55, $p < .005$.

Table 5.2

**Percentage of Youth Answering to the Question
"Do you share your feelings and thoughts with these people?"**

	Kibbutz			Nuclear Family		
	Fathers	Mothers	Friends[a]	Fathers	Mothers	Friends
Often/Sometimes	58.3	66.7	66.7	50	62.5	29.2
Never	41.7	33.3	33.3	50	37.5	70.8
	100	100	100	100	100	100
	(24)	(24)	(24)	(24)	(24)	(24)

a. χ^2 (1, $\underline{N}$ = 48) = 6.76, $\underline{p}$ < .01.

Table 5.3

**Percentage of Youth Answering to the Question
"Do you talk to these people about your future plans?"**

	Kibbutz			Nuclear Family		
	Fathers[a]	Mothers	Friends	Fathers[a]	Mothers	Friends
Often/Sometimes	58.3	58.3	75	29.2	50	58.3
Never	41.7	41.7	25	70.8	50	41.7
	100	100	100	100	100	100
	(24)	(24)	(24)	(24)	(24)	(24)

a. χ^2 (1, $\underline{N}$ = 48) = 4.15, $\underline{p}$ < .05.

Table 5.4

Percentage of Youth Answering to the Question
"When you come across things you do not understand
do these people help you with them?"

	Kibbutz			Nuclear Family		
	Fathers[a]	Mothers[b]	Friends	Fathers[a]	Mothers[b]	Friends
Often/Sometimes	95.8	95.8	83.3	70.8	66.7	70.8
Never	4.2	4.2	16.7	29.2	33.3	29.2
	100	100	100	100	100	100
	(24)	(24)	(24)	(24)	(24)	(24)

a. Fathers, χ^2 $(1, N = 48) = 5.4$, $p < .025$.
b. Mothers, χ^2 $(1, N = 48) = 6.7$, $p < .01$.

Rejection and Support

Rejection and support are important determinants of attachment. Percentage comparisons between nuclear-family and kibbutz youths' perception of the support and rejection they experience from their parents and friends are presented in tables 5.5 and 5.6. Table 5.5 tabulates the answers to the questions, "Do you ever feel unwanted by your father?", "Do you ever feel unwanted by your mother?", and "Do you ever feel unwanted by your friends?" which have been combined into one question, "Do you ever feel unwanted by these people?" By comparison to nuclear-family children, fewer kibbutz children felt unwanted or rejected by their parents (table 5.5). However, these differences were too small to be significant ($p > .05$). Table 5.6 tabulates the answers to three questions asked about fathers, mothers, and friends combined under the heading "Would these people stick by you if you got into bad trouble?"

Table 5.5

**Percentage of Youth Answering to the Question
"Do you ever feel unwanted by these people?"**

	Kibbutz			Nuclear Family		
	Fathers	Mothers	Friends[a]	Fathers	Mothers	Friends
Often/Sometimes	25	41.7	54.3	41.7	54.2	83.3[a]
Never	75	58.3	45.7	58.3	45.8	16.7
	100	100	100	100	100	100
	(24)	(24)	(24)	(24)	(24)	(24)

a. χ^2 $(1, \underline{N} = 48) = 4.75$, $\underline{p} < .05$.

As indicated in table 5.6, significantly $(\underline{p} < .05)$ more kibbutz than nuclear-family children were found to perceive their fathers and mothers as supportive in case of trouble.

Table 5.6

**Percentage of Youth Answering to the Question
"Would these people stick by you if you got into bad trouble?"**

	Kibbutz			Nuclear Family		
	Fathers[a]	Mothers[b]	Friends[c]	Fathers	Mothers	Friends
Certainly/Probably	95.8	100	95.8	58.3	83.3	75
No	4.2	0	4.2	41.7	16.7	25
	100	100	100	100	100	100
	(24)	(24)	(24)	(24)	(24)	(24)

a. Fathers, χ^2 $(1, \underline{N} = 48) = 9.55$, $\underline{p} < .005$.
b. Mothers, χ^2 $(1, \underline{N} = 48) = 4.36$, $\underline{p} < .05$.
c. Friends, χ^2 $(1, \underline{N} = 48) = 4.18$, $\underline{p} < .05$.

Supervision

Hirschi (1969) and Rawls (1971) stress the importance of indirect controls. In the nuclear family, parents usually supervise their children in terms of time allowed away from home, in the choice of their companions, and in various prohibitions they impose. Hirschi (1969) argues that formal surveillance, rules, and restrictions are not sufficient to prevent delinquent acts, since it takes only a few minutes to commit them. At a moment of temptation, parents must be psychologically present in their children's consciousness in order to be included in the potential cost of deviance. In turn, psychological presence appears to be a function of physical distance between parent and child. Children playing in the backyard in their mothers' presence are expected to behave more conventionally than if they were 20 miles away from their mothers in summer camp.[37] For this reason, nuclear-family parents who are away from home working have reduced control and supervision over their children. For similar reasons, Flacks (1978) argues that the nuclear family may no longer be structurally fit to carry out its child-rearing functions.

To the contrary, the kibbutz framework provides for strong informal social controls and supervision. Mothers and fathers may be working, but they are around in the kibbutz and aware of their children's location. Percentage comparisons between nuclear-family and kibbutz children's answers on this topic indicate (table 5.7) that significantly ($p < .05$) more kibbutz children perceive their parents as aware of their whereabouts.

Table 5.7

**Percentage of Youth Answering to the Question
"Do these people know where you are when you are away from home?"**

	Kibbutz			Nuclear	Family	
	Fathers[a]	Mothers[b]	Friends[c]	Fathers	Mothers	Friends
Always/Sometimes	95.8	95.8	95.8	75	62.5	75
Never	4.2	4.2	4.2	25	37.5	25
	100	100	100	100	100	100
	(24)	(24)	(24)	(24)	(24)	(24)

a. Fathers, χ^2 (1, $N = 48$) = 4.18, $p < .05$.
b. Mothers, χ^2 (1, $N = 48$) = 8.08, $p < .005$.
c. Friends, χ^2 (1, $N = 48$) = 4.18, $p < .05$.

Discipline

Inconsistency, anger, and unfairness of parents' discipline result in ambivalence and defiance of authority. Rawls stresses the importance of fair discipline for moral development.[38] "Presumably more development fails to take place to the extent that these conditions are absent, and especially if parental injunctions are not only harsh and unjustified, but enforced by punitive and even physical sanctions" (1971: p. 466).

Devereux and his colleagues (1974) compared kibbutz children's perception of their parents' methods of discipline to that of their friends and *metapelet*. Kibbutz parents were judged least disciplinarian. They may act cold and unfriendly toward the child who misbehaves, but they do not usually impose specific punishment. The *metapelet* was found to be more punitive than kibbutz parents, and comparable to the nuclear-family mother in punitiveness. Similarly, on the basis of his questionnaire results, Spiro (1972) found that kibbutz children expect praise from their parents, blame from the *metapelet*, and a mixture of both from their peers.

Since kibbutz parents do not have the main responsibility of supervision and discipline, their relationships with their children are less troubled with ambivalence and more akin to that of grandparents with their grandchildren. This conclusion was supported by Rabin's study (1965) in which kibbutz children were found to be much less ambivalent toward their parents and to have a more positive attitude toward them than nuclear-family children have toward their own parents.

One may, therefore, conclude that kibbutz communal education, rather than severing the bonds between parents and children, strengthens them. Furthermore, the additional bond created between child and *metapelet* may help neutralize or counterbalance the negative impact of incompetent parents and dilute potential conflicts stemming from them. As in the extended family, kibbutz children could, in case of conflict with their parents, find other possible anchors and support. Margaret Mead (1954) explains the beneficial effects of multiple attachments:

> At present, the specific biological situation of the continuing relationship of the child to its biological mother and its need for care by human beings are being hopelessly confused in the growing insistence that child and biological mother, or mother surrogate, must never be separated, that all separation even for a few days is inevitably damaging, and that if long enough it does irreversible damage . . . . On the contrary, cross-cultural studies suggest that adjustment is most facilitated if the child is cared for by many warm, friendly people. (p. 477)

MORALITY OF ASSOCIATION, COMMITMENT, AND BELIEF

When children reach the morality of association, Rawls' second stage of morality, they belong to various groups—the peer group, the neighborhood, school, and work—within which they learn social cooperation and different social roles and duties. The web of significant relations surrounding them widens.

Like Hirschi (1969), Rawls (1971) stresses the importance of exchange relationships and reciprocity for social cooperation:

> Thus we acquire attachments to persons and institutions according to how we perceive our good to be affected by them. The basic idea is one of reciprocity, a tendency to answer in kind. Now this tendency is a deep psychological fact. Without it our nature would be very different and fruitful social cooperation fragile if not impossible. (pp. 494–495)

Participation in beneficial exchanges allows for new commitments, additional attachments, and new stakes in conformity. The more people realize that their prospects may be jeopardized by deviance, the less likely they will deviate.

The Peer Group

Peer group solidarity is the building block of kibbutz education. From infancy onward, kibbutz children grow up with their peers. Up to first grade, each peer group is usually composed of six children who are taken care of by a *metapelet* and her helper. From first grade through high school, each peer group is expanded to twenty children. The change of sleeping arrangements from communal to familial has not changed the way kibbutz children grow up. Peer group education remains the foundation of kibbutz education. From infancy, horizontal solidarity among peers is stressed in day care, school, the various youth groups, and the Youth Society.

Youngsters rely on each other for companionship and support. The peer group thus constitutes an important source of comfort and security. Its salient rewards are expected to generate a high cost for deviance. As expected, percentage comparisons between kibbutz and nuclear-family children indicate that more kibbutz children respect their friends' opinions (table 5.8), share their feelings and thoughts with their peers (table 5.2), and perceive them as supportive in case of trouble (table 5.6). Furthermore, fewer kibbutz children feel rejected by their peers (table 5.5). All of these comparisons are significant ($p < .05$). The finding that significantly fewer kibbutz than nuclear family children identify with their peers (table 5.1) may also indicate more autonomous and independent behavior on the part of kibbutz children.

Table 5.8

Percentage of Youth Answering to the Question
"Do you respect your best friends' opinion
about the important things in life?"

	Kibbutz	Nuclear Family
	$\underline{n} = 24$	$\underline{n} = 24$
Certainly/Probably	95.8	70.8
Not At All	4.2	29.2
	100	100

χ^2 (1, $\underline{N}$ = 48) = 5.4, $\underline{p}$ < .025.

Group Pressure

The influence of overlapping kibbutz peer groups is tremendous, since there are no alternative groups to which the youth may escape. Being omnipresent, kibbutz peer groups represent a potent means of informal social control and supervision. By contrast, nuclear-family youths who reject or are rejected by one peer group have the choice between finding refuge in another peer group or becoming loners. A percentage comparison between the answers provided by these two groups of children indicate (table 5.7) that significantly ($\underline{p}$ < .05) more kibbutz than nuclear-family children perceive their peers as being aware of their location.

Bettelheim (1969) argues that the kibbutz youth develops a collective superego whose voice is inescapable because the command "you must" issued by the group is related to the threat "We, the group, will cast out anyone who dares deviate." The findings of Devereux and his colleagues (1974) refute this criticism. The kibbutz peer group may act cold, unfriendly, and sometimes refuse to play with the transgressor, but it rarely uses ostracism as a method of discipline. By contrast, exclusion was found to be much more frequent among city youths, who form their peer groups through a process of mutual selection.

Conclusion

Rather than reducing youths' attachment to their parents, kibbutz peer groups provide additional bonds and stakes in conformity and thus become important means of social control. "Children worried about the reactions of their peers tend to have two sources of concern, while those worried first about their parents' reaction tend to have only one" (Hirschi, 1969: p. 149).

KIBBUTZ NEIGHBORHOOD AND PUBLIC OPINION

The kibbutz, characterized by daily face-to-face interaction, actualizes the ideals of mutual help and equality. Operationalization of these ideals consisted in asking kibbutz and nuclear-family children how their families compared to other families in the neighborhood and whether people in the neighborhood care about what happened to them. Percentage comparisons between nuclear-family and kibbutz children, in table 5.9, indicate that significantly ($p < .05$) more kibbutz children perceive kibbutz families as knowing each other and as being of the same economic situation. More kibbutz than nuclear-family children also believe that they are living in a community in which people care for each other ($p < .05$).

Kibbutz youths' attitudes and beliefs about their community are akin to those expected from the people of the well-ordered society:

> A sufficient ground for adopting this duty [mutual aid] is its pervasive effect on the quality of everyday life. The public knowledge that we are living in a society in which we can depend upon others to come to our assistance in difficult circumstances is itself of great value. (Rawls, 1971: p. 339)

In this small community, public opinion, shame, and ridicule are strong means of informal social control. Furthermore, in the kibbutz there are no police. Consequently, by comparison to nuclear-family children, kibbutz children are expected to be more concerned about other adults' opinions than about the police. A percentage comparison between these two groups, in table 5.10, confirms this expectation. Significantly ($p < .05$) more kibbutz than nuclear-family children were found to consider the potential reaction of other adults as the worst thing about getting caught stealing. Furthermore, fear of police treatment does not constitute a threat to kibbutz children as it does for nuclear-family children.

Table 5.9

Percentage of Youth Answering as Indicated
to the Statements

	Kibbutz Family $\underline{n} = 24$	Nuclear Family $\underline{n} = 24$
1. Most of the families in the neighborhood know each other.		
Agree	95.8	62.5
Undecided/Disagree	4.2	37.5
χ^2 (1, $\underline{N}$ = 48) = 8.08, $\underline{p}$ < .005.	100	100
2. How does your family compare with other families in the neighborhood?		
The Same	91.7	58.3
Better off/Worse off	8.3	41.7
χ^2 (1, $\underline{N}$ = 48) = 7.11, $\underline{p}$ < .01.	100	100
3. Most of the people around here do not care about what happens to you.		
Agree	75	45.8
Undecided/Disagree	25	54.2
χ^2 (1, $\underline{N}$ = 48) = 4.38, $\underline{p}$ < .05.	100	100

Table 5.10

**Percentage of Youth Answering as Indicated to the Question
"What is the worst thing about getting caught for stealing?"**

	Kibbutz	Nuclear Family
	$\underline{n} = 24$	$\underline{n} = 24$
Police Treatment[a]	4.2[a]	25
Parents' Anger	12.5	29.2
Friends Look Down on You	37.5	29.2
Other Adults' Reaction[b]	41.7[b]	0
Don't Know	4.2	16.7
	100.1	100.1

a. Police treatment, χ^2 (1, $\underline{N} = 48$) = 21.9, $\underline{p} < .001$.
b. Other adults' reaction, χ^2 (1, $\underline{N} = 48$) = 12.63, $\underline{p} < .001$.

SCHOOL

School is, according to Hirschi (1969), the major institution of social control in the United States. Lack of academic competence, poor school performance, depressed educational aspirations, and dislike for school and teachers are reflected in a lack of commitment and involvement in school. Children with such characteristics stop communicating with their parents, since communicating would mean communicating that they are failures. Bettelheim (1969) and Hirschi (1969) observe that delinquents and dropouts have long before been underachievers.[39] "We have emphasized the fact that a low-status future is not jeopardized by delinquency, that adolescents whose prospects are bleak are to that extent free to commit delinquent acts" (Hirschi, 1969: p. 185). By contrast, kibbutz education, which is based on group performance and evaluation, rejects individual grades as a means of selection and motivation. Classes are set up in cooperative units. Although differences in talent and ability are acknowledged, teachers do not reward or single out top achievers; they encourage students to do their best by contributing to the group's effort, and they reward the group as a whole. In this manner, the academically least advantaged do not lose their self-respect. This may be seen as another consequence of the difference principle. Finally, academic performance is not the only criterion of success. Kibbutz founders, middle-class intellectuals themselves, rejected academic pursuits. Their ideal was to work the earth. Although today kibbutz youths are encouraged to study beyond high school and pursue academic careers, they nevertheless know that whatever the educational level reached, they will find respected work in the kibbutz. Whatever profession chosen, vocational and technical expertise remain valued enterprises. By contrast, for nuclear-family youth formal schooling is the major if not the unique avenue of achievement. A youth without high school diploma has bleak prospects of obtaining a respected position in society.

Kibbutz and nuclear-family children were therefore asked whether it was important to them personally to obtain good grades at school (table 5.11) and whether they thought it was hard to find a job without a high school diploma (table 5.12). Percentage comparisons between kibbutz and nuclear-family children on these dimensions indicate significant differences. Only 20.8 percent of kibbutz children as opposed to 62.5 percent of Israeli nuclear-family children found grades very important (table 5.11). Furthermore, 66.7 percent of Israeli nuclear-family children as opposed to only 25 percent of kibbutz children agreed that without a high school diploma it is hard to find a job (table 5.12).[40]

Table 5.11

Percentage of Youth Answering "Very Important" to the Question "How important is getting good grades to you personally?"

	Kibbutz	Nuclear Family
	$n = 24$	$n = 24$
Very Important	20.8	62.5
Somewhat/Not Important	79.2	37.5
	100	100

χ^2 $(1, N = 48) = 8.57, p < .005.$

Table 5.12

**Percentage of Youth Agreeing with the Statement
"It is hard for young people without
a high school diploma to find a job"**

	Kibbutz	Nuclear Family
	$n = 24$	$n = 24$
Agree	25	66.7
Undecided/Disagree	75	33.3
	100	100

χ^2 (1, $N = 48$) = 8.39, $p < .005$.

Bettelheim (1969) criticized kibbutz education for not allowing its children to fully develop their intellect. Comparing them to nuclear-family children in terms of academic achievement test scores, he found kibbutz youths to cluster in a middle range, the top performers being reduced to this level and the low performers rising to it. He concluded that kibbutz youths are "middle-reachers" in terms of academic competence:

> No doubt the system prevents some from developing as fully as they might, witness the data I have quoted on scholastic achievement. But in sheer numbers they are more than offset by those who (based again on these data) would have achieved much lower were it not for ample support from the group and the educational system. (Bettelheim, 1969: p. 296)

Nevertheless, Bettelheim (1969), as well as Rabin (1965), acknowledge that individual achievement tests based on individual performance are not fair to kibbutz children, who have been socialized within a system that stresses group performance. Within a Rawlsian perspective, this criticism becomes an argument in favor of kibbutz child rearing, since in the original position what matters first and foremost is the improvement of the least advantaged.

Several research findings refute Bettelheim's criticism that cooperative group work lowers top achievers' performance. Davis and Restle (1963) and Shaw (1932) have found group performance to be superior to individual performance on physical and problem-solving tasks. Wodarski, Hamblin, Buckholdt, and Ferritor (1973) devised an experiment that fits the framework of the difference principle. In the experimental group, rewards depended on the average score of the four lowest-performing members of the group, whereas in the control group individual members were rewarded separately for the problems they solved. The average problem-solving accuracy of the experimental group was found to have increased and to have exceeded that of each individual member in the second group. The top achievers in the experimental group were also found to have improved their performance while assisting the lowest performers to improve theirs.

The kibbutz would also encourage talented students to develop their potential, but within constraints similar to those set by the difference principle. For example, if Beethovens were to be found among kibbutz children, they would be sent to the best schools. By developing their talents, these most advantaged children would enrich the group's culture and enhance its members' self-esteem. However, if incurred expenses would cause excessive hardship for the least advantaged and make them worse off than before, then these talented individuals would not be sent to music school. This position is consistent with the notion of justice as fairness. "But the difference principle would allocate resources in education, say, so as to improve the long-term expectation of the least favored. If this end is attained by giving more attention to the better endowed, it is permissible; otherwise not" (Rawls, 1971: p. 101).

Vocational Education and Work

Physical labor and vocational training are integral parts of the kibbutz educational system. When they are 7 years old, kibbutz children work in the children's farm, at 13 years old they work 1 hour and a half per day in the kibbutz farm, and at 17 years old they work there 3 hours a day. Thirteen- to 18-year-old children rotate their location every 3 months in order to experience working in the various branches of the kibbutz economy. By contrast, Israeli nuclear-family children rarely or never work as long as they attend high school. So, when asked whether they worked at least 5 hours a week, all kibbutz, but no nuclear-family children answered affirmatively to this question (table 5.13).

Table 5.13

**Percentage of Youth Working at Least
Five Hours a Week**

	Kibbutz	Nuclear Family
	$n = 24$	$n = 24$
Worked	100	0
Never worked	0	100
	100	100

That physical labor is as valued as intellectual work is consistent with Rawls' theory, since on moral grounds intellectual endeavors are not more worthy than manual ones. Work and vocational training constitute additional avenues of commitment and involvement that could prevent delinquent activities. In Hirschi's (1969) words, "To the extent that he is engrossed in conventional activities, he cannot even think about deviant acts, let alone act out his inclinations" (p. 22).

Unfortunately, in the United States most youngsters are excluded from meaningful work, its rewards, and its penalties. Isolated and alienated from the adult world, they are often deprived of adequate adult role models and authentic responsibilities. Fritz Redl (1965) thus comments, "in contrast to our beautiful sentiments about 'how important' the young are for us, I find, in our society, a lot of 'estrangement' has succeeded in sneaking in between us and the kids we love" (p. 276).

Redl (1965) also describes adolescence as a moratorium without oxygen, in which there is nothing worth doing:

What is the good of a leeway to experiment, when there is nothing for them to experiment with? The urban youngster of my country finds himself in a vehemently infantilized and highly pauperized life-space. His chances for a meaningful work experience, for the opportunity to make a meaningful contribution to society at his own level, are quite poor—and no amount of "recreational facilities" can make up for that fact! (p. 277)

For the same reasons, Goodman (1960) adds that growing up in our industrial society is growing up absurd. Isolation of youth from work creates angry and cynical youngsters with no specific satisfaction but drugs and "conspicuous consumption." Bettelheim (1969) and Riesman (1950) further argue that the hedonistic outlook of many city youth stems in part from their inability to differentiate work from play and production from consumption. Experience with only leisure, play, and consumerism becomes meaningless without the counterpart of this dichotomy—work.

> In fact, we soon realize that the burden put on leisure by the disintegration of work is too huge to be coped with; leisure itself cannot rescue work, but fails with it, and can only be meaningful for most men if work is meaningful, so that the very qualities we looked for in leisure are more likely to come into being there if social and political action fight the two-front battle of work-and-leisure. (Riesman, 1950: p. XLIV)

Not knowing the difference between the essential and the superfluous, nonkibbutz children are hardly ever satisfied. To the contrary, for kibbutz children food is not produced in supermarkets. Working with their parents and other adults, they realize how hard it is to produce the necessary goods for subsistence (Bettelheim, 1969).

BELIEF IN THE MORAL VALIDITY OF THE NORMS

For Rawls (1971) and Hirschi (1969), socialization and the strength of one's beliefs in the moral validity of the social norms vary. For some morality is important, for others it is not. Rawls (1971) states:

> We do not have to contend that everyone, whatever his capacities and desires, has a sufficient reason (as defined by the thin theory) to preserve his sense of justice. For our good depends upon the sorts of persons we are, the kinds of wants and aspirations we have and are capable of. It can even happen that there are many who do not find a sense of justice for their good. (p. 576)

Three Orientations to Delinquency

Kornhauser (1978) argues that there are three orientations to delinquency related to the degree of belief in the moral validity of social norms.[41] At the first orientation, *ambivalence*, delinquents do not challenge the validity of social norms and experience shame and guilt in case of transgression. At the second orientation, *hierarchy of values*, conventional norms are accepted but not all illegal acts are condemned. Finally, at the third orientation to delinquency, *anomie*,[42] the youth is characterized by a total indifference to the social norms. The unattached and normless adopt this attitude.[43] The choice between conformity and deviance is for them a matter of expediency. For Rawls (1971) and Hirschi (1969) anomic individuals lack the characteristics that would make them persons:

> A person who lacks a sense of justice, and who would never act as justice requires except as self-interest and expediency prompt, not only is without ties of friendship, affection, and mutual trust, but is incapable of experiencing resentment and indignation. He lacks certain natural attitudes and moral feelings of a particularly elementary kind. Put another way, one who lacks a sense of justice lacks certain fundamental attitudes and capacities included under the notion of humanity. (Rawls, 1971: p. 488)

Techniques of Rationalization

At the first and second stages of delinquency, youths may use some strategies to lower their belief in the moral validity of the social norms and thus reduce the cost of deviance. Sykes and Matza (1957) call these strategies "techniques of neutralization," and divide them into five categories: (1) denial of responsibility, (2) denial of injury, (3) denial of victim, (4) condemnation of the condemner, and (5) appeal to higher loyalties. Operationalization of these strategies may be found in statements like "It is alright to get around the law if you can get away with it," and "To get ahead you have to do things that are not right." Percentage comparisons between nuclear-family and kibbutz children concerning these techniques of neutralization indicate that by this criterion, the majority of the youths in both groups do not go beyond the first orientation to delinquency. A lower, although not significantly lower ($p > .05$), percentage of kibbutz children adhere to these techniques of neutralization (table 5.14).

Hirschi, however, argues that youngsters who are already delinquent and anomic may use techniques of neutralization as after-the-fact rationalizations, but those who believe in the moral validity of the social norms rarely do. Hirschi (1969) explains:

> Many persons do not have an attitude of respect toward the rules of society; many persons feel no moral obligation to conform regardless of personal advantage. Insofar as the values and beliefs of these persons are consistent with their feelings, and there should be a tendency toward consistency, neutralization is unnecessary; it has already occurred. (p. 25)

Table 5.14

**Percentage of Youth Answering as Indicated
to the Following Statements**

	Kibbutz Family $\underline{n} = 24$	Nuclear Family $\underline{n} = 24$
1. It is alright to get around the law if you can get away with it.		
Agree	12.5	29.2
Undecided/Disagree	87.4	70.8
$\underline{p} > .05$	99.9	100
2. To get ahead one has to do things that are not right.		
Agree	16.7	33.3
Undecided/Disagree	83.3	66.7
$\underline{p} > .05$	100	100
3. Most of the criminals should not be blamed for what they have done.		
Agree	8.3	25
Undecided/Disagree	91.7	75
$\underline{p} > .05$	100	100
4. Most of the things that people call delinquency do not hurt anyone.		
Agree	12.5	33.3
Undecided/Disagree	87.5	66.7
$\underline{p} > .05$	100	100

DELINQUENT ACTS

Hirschi defines delinquency "by acts the detection of which are thought to result in punishment of the person committing them by agents of the larger society" (Hirschi, 1969: p. 47). Within the framework of social control theory, the more the youths are attached, committed, and believe in the moral validity of the social norms, the stronger are their social bonds and the less likely they are to commit delinquent acts. In the present study, more kibbutz than nuclear-family children were found to be attached to the persons and institutions of their society. Kibbutz children had also more avenues of commitment. Having more stakes in conformity, they were expected to commit fewer delinquent acts. Percentage comparisons between nuclear-family and kibbutz children, shown in table 5.15, indicate that fewer ($p < .05$) kibbutz children had taken things that did not belong to them worth less than $5 or worth between $5 and $50. For things worth more than $50, although nuclear-family children took things more often than did kibbutz children, differences between comparison groups have not been found statistically significant.

Percentage comparisons between nuclear family and kibbutz children (table 5.15) indicate that tractors and bicycles are more often taken for a ride without their owners' permission by kibbutz children. Although statistically significant ($p < .05$), these differences are cultural and may be explained by communal ownership. Just as adult kibbutzniks "borrow" a car or a tractor from their kibbutz, kibbutz children "borrow" bicycles and tractors without any thought about theft. In fact, all kibbutz children answered that they always return the "borrowed" items to their owners.

CONCLUSION: OTHER FORMS OF ANOMIC BEHAVIOR

Our findings corroborate with those of Hirschi (1969): children who are attached to many significant others and have various avenues of commitment have additional stakes in conformity and stronger beliefs in the moral validity of the social norms. They are therefore less likely to deviate.

It should be noted that in the present study only one of the possible ways to deviate—delinquency—has been examined. Durkheim (1951), from whom Hirschi (1969) borrowed the concept of anomie, argues that the lack of social integration and regulation could lead not only to crime, but to suicide. When an individual becomes detached from all social groups, his selfish interests prevail.

Table 5.15

Percentage of Youth Answering as Indicated
to the Following Questions

	Kibbutz Family $n = 24$	Nuclear Family $n = 24$
1. Have you ever taken little things worth less than $5 that did not belong to you?		
During last year/More than a year ago	20.8	58.3
Never	79.2	41.7
χ^2 (1, $N = 48$) = 7.06, $p < .01$.	100	100
2. Have you ever taken things of some value (between $5 and $50) that did not belong to you?		
During last year/More than a year ago	4.2	25
Never	95.8	75
χ^2 (1, $N = 48$) = 4.18, $p < .05$.	100	100
3. Have you ever taken things of large value worth more than $50 that did not belong to you?		
During last year/More than a year ago	0	12.5
Never	100	87.5
χ^2 (1, $N = 48$) = 3.2, $p > .05$.	100	100

Table 5.15 (cont.)

	Kibbutz Family $n = 24$	Nuclear Family $n = 24$
4. Have you ever taken a car for a ride without its owner's permission?		
During last year/More than a year ago	8.3	25
Never	91.7	75
χ^2 (1, N = 48) = 2.4, p > .05.	100	100
5. Have you ever taken a tractor for a ride without its owner's permission?		
During last year/More than a year ago	37.5	0
Never	62.5	100
χ^2 (1, N = 48) = 11.08, p < .001.	100	100
6. Have you ever taken a bike for a ride without its owner's permission		
During last year/More than a year ago	58.3	29.2
Never	41.7	70.8
χ^2 (1, N = 48) = 4.14, p < .05.	100	100
7. Whenever you take something that does not belong to you do you bring it back?		
Always	100	83.3
Sometimes/Never	0	16.7
χ^2 (1, N = 48) = 4.36, p < .05.	100	100

Binding social and individual disintegration together, Durkheim (1951) remarks:

> But society cannot disintegrate without the individual simultaneously detaching himself from social life, without his own goals becoming preponderant over those of the community . . . . The more weakened the groups to which he belongs, the less he depends on them, the more he consequently depends only on himself and recognizes no other rules of conduct than what are founded on his private interests. (p. 209)

In times of melancholy and despair, individuals with no bonds or commitment often commit suicide. "So far as they are the admitted masters of their destinies, it is their privilege to end their lives" (Durkheim, 1951: p. 209). During social deregulation, which Durkheim (1951) attributes to the disappearance of religion, the emergence of industry, and sudden economic prosperity, individuals may become anomic. No longer accepting social norms as regulating their desires, aspirations, or actions, their passions become unleashed, their goals become infinite. Earning a living becomes greed. "From top to bottom of the ladder, greed is aroused without knowing where to find ultimate foothold" (Durkheim, 1951: p. 256). Love without social regulation becomes unlimited lust. The result is despair and meaninglessness—the outcome is often suicide (Durkheim, 1951).[44]

Cloward and Ohlin (1960), two strain theorists, also mention that besides gravitating toward crime and delinquency, those who drop out of every opportunity structure may drift to a lower-class life style, a retreatist subculture, or drugs. President Bush's (1991) statement reflects the same perspective:

> People think the problem in our world is crack, or suicide, or babies having babies; and those are the symptoms. The disease is a kind of moral emptiness, though. And we cannot continue producing generations born numbly into despair, finding solace in a needle or a vial. If, as president, I had the power to give just one thing to this great country, it would be the return of an inner moral compass, nurtured by the family and valued by society. (Bush, quoted in Office of Juvenile Justice and Delinquency Prevention: Annual Report, 1991: p. 5)

Thus, delinquency is only one of the many manifestations of anomic behavior. Child abuse, skinheads, drugs, divorce, alienation, suicide, cults, conspicuous consumption, hedonism, sadism, racism, and anti-Semitism are other symptoms of its presence.

Chapter 6

Moral Autonomy

By being attached to their parents and friends, and having various avenues of commitment, kibbutz children have been found to have more stakes in conformity and to commit fewer delinquent acts than nuclear-family children. The question that has yet to be answered is whether kibbutz children are more morally developed than nuclear-family children, or as Bettelheim (1969) has argued, only more conforming due to stronger indoctrination.[45]

Bettelheim (1969) has characterized kibbutz children up to 13 years of age as *The Children of the Dream*. They are able to develop psychomotor skills without experiencing intense conflicts or tensions and to grow without too many frustrations or demands. They can freely explore their environment and develop a strong sense of industry. But thereafter, they stagnate. They lack individuality, autonomy, and flexibility in thought and action. They are overconforming, flat in affect, and unable to form intimate relationships. Adopting a psychoanalytic orientation, Bettelheim attributes these drawbacks to the kibbutz practice of raising children in groups away from their parents.

BETTELHEIM'S CRITICISMS OF KIBBUTZ EDUCATION

One of Bettelheim's major criticisms of kibbutz education was that kibbutz children cannot experience intimacy or develop a sense of uniqueness because they have never felt totally dependent and attached to one person, their mothers, as is the case with nuclear-family children. Peer group education prevents them from developing a sense of exclusive belonging which is at the root of intimate relationships. The strong feeling of belonging to a group cannot compensate for this lack:

> But for us in the West, I believe that we all wish to be terribly important
> to someone . . . . But this is very different from being important to some
> hundred persons as a member of their community. In modern Western
> society, this not being very important to the whole community is our loss;
> being extremely important to a very few (if we are) is our gain.
> (Bettelheim, 1969: p. 252)

Kibbutz children are also "flat in affect" because they never experienced
all the nuances of emotions learned by being close and attuned to one person.
Furthermore, kibbutz children never had the opportunity to express intense
negative feelings toward their parents or peers. The limited time spent with
their parents and the strong dependency on the group prevent them from
doing so.

Another drawback of kibbutz education is that kibbutz children are
socialized by the peer group and not by their parents. As a result, they
develop a collective ego rather than a personal autonomous ego and
superego, which stunts individuality:

> [The collective superego] will not need to develop great complexity or
> richness. While very strong by comparison, it will (again by comparison)
> be considerably less personalized. Because above all, the voice of such a
> collective superego is also the voice of the external environment.
> (Bettelheim, 1969: p. 130)

Being continually among peers prevents kibbutz children from adopting
new values they would oppose to those of the group in order to define
themselves. Kibbutz children also lack a sense of personal identity because
they have never experienced the conflict between being themselves and being
enmeshed in a group. Kibbutz children are really themselves only when they
are with others. "Together they can all feel, act, be; alone by themselves,
they seem to have very little capacity for any of these" (Bettelheim, 1969:
p. 263).

Finally, Bettelheim' argued that kibbutz youths lack of the kind of
flexibility that would enable them to adapt to new situations. "They are
lacking in that immediate and flexible evaluation, a spontaneous adjustment
to ever-changing situations that make for the most useful soldier today"
(1969: p. 264).

REFUTATION OF BETTELHEIM'S CRITICISM

Numerous research findings based on a variety of research designs refute
Bettelheim's criticism. The study of Devereux and his colleagues (1974), as
well as ours, indicates that by comparison to nuclear-family children, kibbutz

youngsters were not less but more attached to their parents. And even though kibbutz parents do not directly provide for their children's needs, they offer them strong emotional support. They may also be expected to treat their children as unique individuals.

According to Freud, the nuclear-family child's conscience or superego is formed with the resolution of the oedipal conflict achieved by defensive identification with the opposite-sex parent. The male child introjects the image of his father and becomes, in a way, his father in order to follow his precepts. The more intense the oedipal conflict, the stronger the identification with the father and the stronger the superego. However, the stronger the superego, the more irrational, blind, and punitive it may become.

By contrast, the development of the kibbutz child's conscience is not based on constraint and authority, but on cooperation tempered by the give and take of equals. Consequently, the oedipal conflict is less intense. Rabin (1965), who examined nuclear-family and kibbutz children on Rorschach tests and sentence completions, found that kibbutz children experience less conflict toward their parents and represent them less often in fantasy. Similarly, Devereux and his colleagues (1974) found kibbutz children to be less ambivalent about their parents than nuclear-family children, while Jarus and his colleagues (1970) found them to be less neurotic and to exhibit a stronger and more wholesome personality.

The studies of Amir (1969) and Kahane (1975) have disconfirmed Bettelheim's conclusion about kibbutz youths' lack of flexibility and adaptation to new situations:

> Secondly, these youths seem to display a large capacity for innovation and flexible adaption in adjusting to changing physical and social conditions. This capacity has been revealed in an active adaption to day-to-day reality—a style in which one activates all the resources at one's disposal in order to cope with different situations and current problems. (Kahane, 1975: p. 344)

Bettelheim's criticism concerning kibbutz adolescents' lack of individuality has also been refuted. Jay and Birney (1973) tested kibbutz and moshav[46] adolescents on the Marlowe-Crowne Social Desirability Scale and found that moshav adolescents have a greater fear of failure and a greater need for social approval than kibbutz children:

> In other words, contrary to the prediction, the moshav adolescent reports himself as the more anxious to include others in his activities . . . . [He or she] experiences a greater pressure from his environment than does the kibbutz adolescent. (Jay & Birney, 1973: pp. 352, 354)

Rabin (1965) also found kibbutz adolescents to be relatively free from the conflicts and stresses experienced by nonkibbutz adolescents and concluded that kibbutz youths must have become independent at a much earlier age than nuclear-family children.[47] Egalitarian peer group interactions seem to stimulate kibbutz adolescents to grow and to explore new aspects of their personality.

With the increase in familism, as seen in the change in sleeping arrangements, kibbutz youths are less likely to be constantly submerged in or by the group. They have the opportunity to develop their individuality while being treated as unique individuals by their parents and their siblings with whom they can spend the evening hours at home.

THE FAMILY: INADEQUATE MILIEU FOR MORAL DEVELOPMENT

Throughout history many philosophers and social scientists have rejected the family as an adequate milieu for the development of a strong sense of community and morality. The warmth, intimacy, and mutual accommodation that characterize family relationships do not allow for cooperation through regulation and cannot teach the imperative character of rule or duty. Durkheim (1961) argues, "the child must learn respect for the rule; he must learn to do his duty because it is his duty, because he feels obligated to do so even though the task may not seem an easy one" (pp. 147–148).

Durkheim (1961) also adds that children will learn commitment to collective goals only when they are freed from the individualistic solitary familial upbringing and allowed to participate in collective life:

> To learn the love of collective life we must live it not only in our minds and imagination, but in reality. It is not enough to form in a child the potential for attaching himself to the group. We must stimulate this power by effective experience. For only thus can it shape and be strengthened. (Durkheim, 1961: p. 220)

Similarly, to enhance community feelings rather than particularistic ties that would generate envy and jealousy, Plato (1965, bk. 5) recommended that the guardians of the state be raised in a group away from their families. Not knowing their parents, they would not experience egoistic or particularistic relationships leading to a society split into mine and yours. Finally, Kohlberg (1971) notes that maximum warmth and affection in the nuclear-family setting is not conducive to optimum moral development.

To achieve the ideals of equality and social cooperation, kibbutz education focuses on peer socialization. Although kibbutz children no longer sleep at the children's house but at their parents' homes, they spend the great majority of their waking hours in nurseries, schools, and other communal enterprises. Being most of the time among peers, their experience with hierarchical relations found among family members is minimal. Reciprocal relations with their peers allow them to transform their perception of rules in a way nuclear-family children are unable to do (Piaget, 1966).[48]

KOHLBERG'S THEORY OF MORAL DEVELOPMENT

Basing his theory on the work of Piaget (1966), Kohlberg (1971) adopted a cognitive-developmental approach to morality. In this model, moral development goes through three invariant universal levels, each including two stages.[49]

Level I, the preconventional level, corresponds to Rawls' morality of authority and is typical of children 4 to 10 years of age and of delinquents. At *stage one* moral conflicts are solved in terms of might makes right, and seem to encapsulate Callicles' answer in Plato's dialogue *Gorgias* that might is right, and that law is nothing but the ruling of the many weak over the few strong (Plato, 1979, sec. 482-486). At *stage two* conflicts are solved in terms of hedonistic exchange. Fairness is defined as exchanges that bring pleasant results, "You scratch my back and I'll scratch yours."

Level II, the conventional level of morality, corresponds to Rawls' morality of association. At this level one adopts the perspective of law and order. Moral conflicts are solved within a societal frame of reference. Most people operate at this level. At *stage three* conflicts are solved by reference to conventional definitions of good. Action is motivated by a strong need for approval. At *stage four* conflicts are solved in terms of legitimation of conventional values and support of societal order.

Level III is the postconventional level of morality. At this level values and principles acquire validity independent of social allegiances. At *stage five* one adopts a social contract view, which is utilitarian and emphasizes procedural rules. Right action is defined in terms of individual rights. At *stage six* moral conflicts are solved by going back to the original position and accepting universal principles such as the sacredness of human life and the difference principle. Kohlberg's last level of moral development is equivalent to Rawls' morality of principles and embodies the concept of justice as fairness. Only a small percentage of individuals reach stages five or six. The majority of people remain at the second level of morality, stages three and four.

RELATION BETWEEN KOHLBERG'S AND RAWLS' THEORIES

Kohlberg's and Rawls' theories interrelate in several ways. Through ideal roletaking and empathy, Kohlberg reaches the same principles of justice as Rawls, who starts with self-interested, mutually disinterested individuals under the veil of ignorance. Both situations result in the committment to the difference principle and in the readiness to live by this principle no matter what the individual's social position is, and even after some find out that they are among the most advantaged. The interrelations between Rawls' and Kohlberg's theories are such that empirical studies and scientific research methods are able to provide support to philosophical theories. Conversely, Kohlberg appeals to Rawls' theory to elucidate the sixth stage of moral development:

> The tradition of moral philosophy to which we appeal is the liberal or rational tradition, in particular the "formalistic" or "deontological" tradition running from Immanuel Kant to John Rawls. Central to this tradition is the claim that an adequate morality is *principled*, i.e., that it makes judgments in terms of *universal* principles applicable to all mankind. (Kohlberg, 1975: p. 672)

Rawls agrees with Kohlberg that the superiority of a theory is not a psychological but a philosophical question:

> It is true that I argue for the theory of justice as superior, and work out the psychological theory of this presumption; but this superiority is a philosophical question and cannot, I believe, be established by the psychological theory of development alone. (Rawls, 1971: p. 462, n. 8)

The perspective of this book is that philosophical theories and social science findings ought to support each other in a process of reflective equilibrium. A philosophical model should be able to cast light upon and provide justification for psychological and educational theories and findings. On the other hand, to be more than a logical possibility, that is, socially and psychologically feasible, philosophical theories should be consistent with social science findings. Rawls' model of justice and Kohlberg's theory and findings do, in this way, provide each other balance and support.

LACK OF SOCIAL BONDS: STUNTED MORAL DEVELOPMENT

Like Rawls and Hirschi, Kohlberg (1971) and his colleagues found social bonds to be a precondition for moral development. Communication breakdown and lack of participation and integration in social groups prevent the move from the preconventional to the conventional level of morality. "If the child has not experienced a trustworthy relationship and does not see himself as a member of a coherent society or group, then he cannot understand the shared norms and values that underlie conventional moral thought" (Gilligan, 1980: p. 505).

In one study (Kohlberg, 1971), 83 percent of the delinquents interviewed were found to be at the preconventional level of moral development. Moreover, institutionalized children growing up in a cold and impersonal environment have been found lacking even the minimal intellectual stimulation necessary to reach preconventional moral thinking (Timm, 1981). They were at stage zero, even below delinquents' stage of moral development. This stage is characterized by a total lack of awareness of authority and a total absence of patterns of reward and punishment.

DEVELOPMENT OF COMPLEX COGNITIVE STRUCTURES AND MORAL DEVELOPMENT

The advance to higher stages of morality requires the development of complex cognitive structures, which include the operations of equality and reciprocity and culminate in Rawls' original position (Kohlberg, 1975). For instance, at stage two, reciprocity is interpreted as an obligation to return favors. At stage three, reciprocity is not only in deeds but in perspective. One attempts to coordinate one's perspective with that of others. Finally, at stage six, one acquires the ability to trade places with others, assume their roles, and adopt their point of view:

> We must recognize that these different points of view exist, that the perspectives of others are not the same as ours. But we must not only learn that things look different to them, but they have different wants and ends, and different plans and motives. (Rawls, 1971: pp. 468–469)

CROSS-CULTURAL STUDIES ON MORAL DEVELOPMENT

Gilligan (1980) points out that adolescents who do not experience an environment in which values sometimes clash cannot develop beyond conventional morality. For instance, Turiel, Edwards, and Kohlberg (1978) and Turiel (1980) found that Turkish children who grow up in a homogeneous village are unable to develop beyond the conventional stages of morality.

To the contrary, kibbutz children do not grow up in groups that are isolated from the rest of the world, as Bettelheim seemed to have implied. They meet with many city youngsters in various youth movements. Mass media and travel in Israel and abroad widen their view of the world and stimulate their moral development. Kibbutz adolescents may often go through a phase of ethical relativism in which they question the values of the kibbutz and oppose them to those of Israeli society. They may also criticize their parents, but unlike nuclear-family adolescents, they do not feel alienated from them. They usually outgrow this phase by rethinking, rediscovering anew, and integrating as their own kibbutz principles and values. Kohlberg (1971) states:

> But the adolescent must make or remake ideologies for himself to really arrive at moral principles. Or to put it differently, to reach full maturity he must differentiate the kibbutz ideology or way of life from the basic universal moral principles on which that way of life rests. (p. 367)

Therefore, the multiple agents of socialization and the rich sociocultural environment of the kibbutz provide the youth a variety of perspectives and moral exemplars.

Kohlberg's studies and those of his colleagues on moral development of youth in Turkey, Israel, Taiwan, Great Britain, and Honduras help determine whether the kibbutz society stimulates autonomous moral behavior or merely more conformism. Bar-Yam, Kohlberg, and Naame (1980), Kohlberg (1971), and Reimer (1972) compared the moral development of kibbutz and city youths of various countries by asking them to solve six moral dilemmas. In each of these dilemmas the value of life is opposed to another value. For instance, in the Heinz Dilemma, the wife of Heinz is very sick and will die if he does not steal the expensive drug he cannot afford to buy and that the druggist does not want to give to him. Two other dilemmas are the Drowning Man Dilemma and the Captain Dilemma.

Moral Maturity Scores (MMS) were then computed by averaging the scores the youth has obtained on each one of the six dilemmas. "The MMS is the sum of the percent usage of each stage weighted or multiplied by the ordinal value of that stage from one to six. These scores then may range from 100 (100 percent stage 1) to 600 (100 percent stage 6)" (Bar-Yam, Kohlberg, & Naame, 1980: p. 349). Table 6.1 shows the Moral Maturity Scores that youths from various countries and socioeconomic status obtained. Kibbutz youths' Moral Maturity Score was 415, as opposed to 374 MMS for middle-class city Israeli children, and 347 MMS for U.S. middle-class children. Thus, by comparison to Israeli and U.S. nuclear-family youths, kibbutz youths were found to be not merely more conforming to the social norms, but more autonomous in their moral behavior and more principled in their reasoning.

Table 6.1

**Moral Maturity Score (MMS) and Percentage Usage
of Each Moral Stage by Various Groups**

GROUP	S	T	A	G	E	S		
	1	2	3	4	5	5B	6	MMS
ISRAEL								
Kibbutz-Born	-	-	14	47	28	11	-	415
Middle Class	-	1	27	65	5	2	-	374
Lower Class	16	21	28	35	0	-	-	289
Youth Aliyah	-	2	33	45	15	5	-	376
UNITED STATES								
Middle Class	0	13	32	50	5	-	-	347
Working Class	8	20	29	42	1	-	-	308
Disadvantaged	12	24	35	28	1	-	-	246
GREAT BRITAIN								
Middle Class	5	23	43	21	8	-	2	313
Working Class	27	44	22	6	0	-	0	209
TURKEY								
Middle Class	10	15	51	24	0	-	0	289
Lower Class	12	32	48	8	0	-	0	252

Note: Stage 5B includes all those adolescents in transition
toward the last stage of moral development.
Source: Bar-Yam, Kohlberg, & Naame, 1980: p. 351.

MORAL DEVELOPMENT OF UNDERPRIVILEGED CITY
CHILDREN GROWING UP IN THE KIBBUTZ

The moral development of underprivileged children placed in the kibbutz through the Youth Aliyah/Chevrot Noar program has also been examined by Kohlberg and his associates (an explanation of this program may be found in chapter 4). Kohlberg (1971) remarked that "many of these adolescents, however, are cognitively and socially disadvantaged; i.e., they are retarded in cognitive and social development due to deprivations and stresses of one sort or another" (p. 352).

In spite of these initial disadvantages, the kibbutz environment was found to stimulate the cognitive and moral development of these Youth Aliyah children (Bar-Yam, Kohlberg, & Naame, 1980). When compared to the lower-class control group they originate from, Youth Aliyah children, after living two years in the kibbutz, significantly ($\underline{p} < .05$) improved their MMS. The MMS score they obtained was 376, as opposed to the MMS of 289 of the lower-class control group; which constituted an improvement of 87 points. Kohlberg (1971) comments:

> Of major and central interest is the comparison of the Youth Aliyah boys and those from the lower-class living in the city . . . . It is not only significantly higher than the city lower-class group (in the statistical sense), but it is dramatically higher. In contrast to the city lower-class, the kibbutz-placed boys show almost no preconventional (stage 1 and 2) thinking, while over one-third of the city lower-class thinking is preconventional. (p. 350)

Bar-Yam, Kohlberg, and Naame (1980) also point out that "whereas 37 percent of the reasoning of the city Oriental boys is at the two preconventional stages, only 2 percent of the Youth Aliyah reasoning was at the two preconventional stages" (p. 352). The MMS of Youth Aliyah children was found to be similar to that of middle-class Israeli children (376 MMS versus 374 MMS), and higher than that of U.S. middle-class children (376 MMS versus 347 MMS).

Opposed to cultural and moral relativism, Gilligan (1980) and Kohlberg (1971) concluded that by the concept of justice they embody, some cultures, such as the kibbutz, provide more role-taking opportunities and are thus more conducive to cognitive and moral development. The question then becomes, What factors and institutions peculiar to kibbutz communal child rearing stimulate moral growth and prosocial behavior?

FACTORS STIMULATING MORAL GROWTH IN THE KIBBUTZ

Competitive versus Cooperative Reward Structure

Kibbutz and nuclear-family norms and values seem antithetical. The kibbutz emphasizes social responsibility and group achievement. The nuclear family stresses competition and individual achievement. Competitive reward structures often encourage lack of cooperation and antisocial behavior because when individuals compete for the same goals, one person's gains become another person's losses (Bronfenbrenner, 1970; Eiferman, 1970; Nadler, Romek, & Shapira-Friedman, 1979; Shapira & Madsen, 1969).

Bronfenbrenner (1970) criticizes the educational orientation in the United States that pushes students to excel with a total disregard for social responsibility and others' welfare. *Time* magazine's report (1974: p. 62) of the "academic guerilla war" of pre-med students who tear pages from library books and refuse to help each other is reminiscent of Rawls' concept of the private society, in which "no one takes account of the good of others or what they possess; rather everyone prefers the most efficient scheme that gives him the largest share of assets" (Rawls, 1971: p. 521).

Mutual Help and Social Responsibility

By contrast, the kibbutz values of mutual help and social cooperation are more akin to Rawls' ideal of a social union:

> There must be an agreed scheme of conduct in which the excellences and enjoyments of each are complementary to the good of all. Each can then take pleasure in the actions of the others as they jointly execute a plan acceptable to everyone . . . . When this end is achieved, all find satisfaction in the very same thing; and this fact together with the complementary nature of the good of individuals affirms the tie of community. (Rawls, 1971: p. 526)

Kibbutz children are encouraged to be socially responsible. The highest achievements in their society are working well together, the attainment of esprit de corps, and good comradeship. Competitive drives are not suppressed but rechanneled toward collective goals. The following studies show how this occurs.

Starting with the hypothesis that the games children play reflect the values of their society, Eiferman (1970) found that kibbutz children mostly played two-party games, such as volleyball or basketball, which allowed for competition between groups coupled with cooperation within each group:

It turns out that exclusively cooperative games, the single party games, are scarcely played at all amongst kibbutz children while group games which demand cooperation towards the achievement of a common aim, but within an overall competitive framework, are far more popular amongst these children. (Eiferman, 1970: p. 585)

Shapira and Madsen (1969) compared kibbutz children's moves on the Madsen Game Board to those of Israeli nuclear-family children.[50]

Nuclear-family children were found to continue to compete even when it was no longer in their self-interest to do so. To the contrary, when told to compete, kibbutz children set rules of cooperation and worked as a team. Shapira and Madsen (1969) explain that early on, at the toddler's house, the unproductive competition to monopolize the attention of the *metapelet* leads to the internalization of the values of sharing and cooperation that is so essential for group life. "When cooperative behavior was adaptive, children of the kibbutz were generally able to cooperate successfully for maximum performance, whereas urban children were usually not able to do so" (Shapira & Madsen, 1969: p. 617).

Finally, Nadler, Romek, and Shapira-Friedman (1979) found kibbutz children to score higher than nuclear-family children on the Attitude Social Responsibility Scale (ASRS), which "measures the degree to which an individual believes he should take upon himself group goals and fulfill them reliably and loyally" (1979: p. 61). When faced with the choice of keeping the coins received for correctly solving problems or donating them to needy children, the majority of kibbutz children agreed to donate their coins to more needy children.

THE YOUTH SOCIETY: A DEMOCRATIC EGALITARIAN ENVIRONMENT

To fully understand the kibbutz educational system and why it comes so close to Rawls' ideals, one must examine a structure unique to the kibbutz educational system: the Youth Society. This is a miniature copy of the adult society, with the same democratic principles. Semi-autonomous, the Youth Society has its general assembly and various committees in which every adolescent participates. Within this framework, the youths work, practice sports, go on field trips, and participate in many other organized activities. The *madrich* (guide) is the only adult authorized to intervene in order to guide the group toward greater cooperation (Kahane, 1975: p. 352, n. 12). Symmetrical egalitarian relations are emphasized, and adolescents are encouraged to discuss the problems and conflicts they face in real-life situations. Kahane (1975) states, "thus, in a system of symmetrical interaction, kibbutz youth learns and commits itself to the norm of reciprocity—that is, to more universal values" (p. 345).

In this forum, rules and procedures are formulated and tested. This process enhances group solidarity and a sense of community:

> Furthermore, within their "mini-society" children were given the opportunity to experiment through the process of trial and error in a framework which was semi-serious and semi-game like, i.e., in a context which might be defined as structural moratorium. In this context, youths test the application of different rules and modes of behaviour before committing themselves to specific value patterns and role models. (Kahane, 1975: pp. 346–347)

Any matter of unfairness is discussed and resolved through the democratic process of the Youth Society's general assembly. Refusal to perform one's duty or carry out one's responsibilities is brought to its attention. The reprimanded youths will be criticized and pressured, but persuasion comes from equals. The "delinquent" youth may respond to accusations without feeling inferior or intimidated, as many adolescents do when they have to answer to their parents. Furthermore, kibbutz youths do know how much their peers also transgress. Peers are not placed on a pedestal as are nuclear-family parents. Youths who have transgressed a norm thus realize how easily they could catch up. These dynamics strengthen the bonds between members of the Youth Society and create a strong sense of community:

> As we have noted, a more unconditional caring for our good and a clearer refusal by others to take advantage of accident and happenstance, must strengthen our self-esteem; and this greater good must in turn lead to a closer affiliation with persons and institutions by way of an answer in kind. (Rawls, 1971: p. 499)

Based on the previous research findings, it may be inferred that kibbutz children's patterns of behavior are not the result of group pressure and indoctrination. They arise from modeling, caring, and solidarity with other group members. Bar-Yam, Kohlberg, and Naame (1980) thus concluded that the kibbutz adult and youth societies represent ideal environments for developing a sense of justice. "It seems that the kibbutz does provide a stimulating environment for moral development, both because of its educational system and the example presented to the youth by the adult society" (p. 356).

Individual versus Group Commitment

Not only is the Youth Society a fertile ground for the exercise of solidarity, mutual help, and responsibility, it also allows for the respect of individuality. In this milieu the conflict between individual and group commitment or individual and collective goals is resolved. Aspiring to live a life based on friendship and cooperation, the youth understands that concern for other members and oneself are united into a common desire. In his vision of a just society, Rousseau expresses the same ideas:

> The better the state is constituted, the more public affairs take precedence over private business in the minds of the citizens. There is, in fact, much less private business, because the sum of private happiness, so that he has less portion of each individual's happiness, so that he has less of it to seek by private means. (Rousseau, 1947: bk. 3, chap. 15)

Similarly, Rawls' (1971) concept of social union encapsulates the complementary nature of individual and collective goods. "Different persons with similar or complementary capacities may cooperate so to speak in realizing their common or matching nature" (pp. 522–523).

Being committed to a community that has become part of themselves, kibbutz adolescents were found to excel in tasks that combine individual success with group responsibility. Devereux and his colleagues (1974) point out that the kibbutz educational system is "capable of producing not only committed, cooperative kibbutzniks, but also a very large share of the nation's political and military leadership" (1974: p. 280).

Kohlberg (1971) also comments on the sense of meaning and deep commitment to the group that Youth Aliyah children have developed by participating in the Youth Society:

> They expressed the security a stable morally-oriented peer group provided them. They expressed the security of knowing what they wanted to be in life and their ability to be it. They expressed the sense of meaning which they felt being a member of a committed community would provide. (p. 371)

These findings were so impressive that Kohlberg (1975) proposed to create kibbutzim in the Untied States in order to help disadvantaged youth and bridge the gap between moral thought and action.[51]   "A participatory democracy provides more extensive opportunities for role taking and a higher level of perceived institutional justice than does any other social arrangement" (p. 676).

CONCLUSION

The empirical findings of Kohlberg (1971), Bar-Yam, Kohlberg, & Naame (1980), Gilligan (1980), Devereux and his colleagues (1974), Reimer (1972), Rabin (1965), Kahane (1975), Shapira and Madsen (1969), and Eiferman (1970), as well as ours, lead to the conclusion that kibbutz children exhibit principled autonomous moral thinking and behavior rarely present among nuclear-family children. Kibbutz child-rearing practices thus provide the opportunity for social participation and stimulate its youth to adopt the standpoint of justice. Given all of this, it would then follow that, by comparison to those of the nuclear family, kibbutz communal child-rearing practices are more congruent with Rawls' *Theory of Justice*, and therefore should be adopted among the basic institutions of the well-ordered society.

Chapter 7

Implications for Americans

One may wonder, What are the implications that flow from this research for Americans interested in pursuing justice for children? The kibbutz may be unique to Israel, but the similarities between the changes the family structure in America and Israel are undergoing and the way people live in both countries invite comparisons. Israelis not only have strong ties to America, they also face comparable problems.

In both countries, the benefits of industrialization failed to "trickle down" to poor urban areas plagued by unemployment, broken families, illiteracy, and semiliteracy. Ethnic division, such as between Askenazi and Sepharadic peoples in Israel, confound the problems. Over 400,000 refugees from Arab countries arrived in Israel between 1948 and 1951, when the new state's population doubled.[52] These Sepharadic Jews did not successfully compete with approximately the same number of Askenazi Holocaust survivors arriving from Europe. Shortages in housing and employment as well as normative clash between the Sepharadic and European cultures undermined Sepharadic patriarchal tradition. For three generations, Sepharadic people have remained Israel's disenfranchised underclass. However, ethnic and class divisions are not as devastating as the white/black and the rich/poor schisms in the United States. Intermarriage between Askenazi and Sepharadic is now common and generally accepted, and there is much more intermingling and cooperation between groups, such as in the reserves, in wartime, and against terrorist wars of attrition.

Moreover, the kibbutz has been found to be an ideal natural environment for valid cross-cultural comparisons having practical consequences for each culture. Leviatan (1973), director of the Center for Research on the Kibbutz, reports that the findings on the kibbutz corroborate with those in other settings:

The relationships among organizational, psychological, and behavioral variables found in our study have also been found in Europe and in the United States . . . . This is very encouraging to a social scientist because it means two things: kibbutz researchers may consider social, psychological and organizational theories developed in the Western world as valid tools to be used within the kibbutz framework; and the outside world may use kibbutz society as a natural laboratory and gain from its experiences ideas relevant to its own conduct. (p. 171)

THREATS TO CHILDREN'S WELL-BEING

Among the disenfranchised in the United States, the number of abused, neglected, and delinquent children is increasing. In 1990, there were five times more reports of sexual maltreatment in the United States than in 1976.[53]

Teen victimizations are most likely to occur in or around schools. The results of a survey conducted from 1985 to 1988 indicate that 37 percent of violent victimization of youths between 12 and 15 years of age occurred in or around schools (Allen-Hagen & Sickmund, 1993). In 1990, one out of five high school students reported carrying a weapon somewhere at least once during the past month (Allen-Hagen & Sickmund, 1993).

Gang- and drug-related murders have become so common that some inner city schools must teach students how to grieve the death of a family member (Doherty, 1989: p. 73). Schools may also provide psychological first aid after violent attacks (Seltzner, 1992), or conduct shooting drills (Terry, 1992: p. A-6) to teach students how to lie down on the floor to avoid bullets. Brutal crimes are committed by younger and younger sociopaths, who seem very respected by their peers.[54]

From 1980 to 1990, the percentage of 1 to 14 year old children who died from homicide increased by 21 percent (*Kids Count*, 1993: p. 25). In 1990, homicide and legal intervention was the fourth leading cause of death of children 1 to 4 years of age, and the third leading cause of death of youths 5 to 14 years of age.[55] Between 1987 and 1991, the number of Violent Crime Index arrests of juveniles increased by 50 percent, which is twice the increase of the adult rate (Allen-Hagen & Sickmund, 1993). Juvenile arrest for murder increased by 85 percent during this time period, in comparison to the 21 percent increase for adults. In the National Crime Victimization Surveys of 1985–1988, youths under 20 years of age who constituted only 14 percent of the survey population were found to account for 30 percent of violent crime victimization (Allen-Hagen & Sickmund, 1993). In a study of twelve countries considered comparable to the United States, male youths were murdered at least five times more frequently in America than in the other countries of comparison except Mexico (Hobbs & Lippman, 1990: p. 112).

The psychological damage of violence has far reaching consequences for children. Children experiencing domestic violence in their home and/or neighborhood cannot feel safe and secure and cannot trust themselves or their environment (Wallach, 1993). They are at risk of modeling violent behavior (Wallach, 1993). They may feel worthless and guilty of being the cause of violent incidents at home (Hetherton, Cox, & Cox, 1982; Wallerstein & Kelly, 1980), or helpless and angry (Terr, 1983; Wallach, 1993). They often exhaust their cognitive energy building defenses against dangers, with no energy left for learning (Terr, 1981).

The fear of child abduction is haunting every concerned parent, and child pornography has become epidemic (*Child Pornography and Pedophilia*, 1986). The director of a missing children's organization states that no child is safe: "Don't let your children go anywhere alone. Our society is breaking down" (McBride, cited in Van Biema, 1993: p. 31).

Kolata (1989) also reports that "crack is rapidly accelerating the destruction of families in poor urban neighborhoods where mothers are becoming increasingly addicted and children are selling the drugs in greater number than ever before" (p. A-1). She goes on to describe the routine selling of young girls into prostitution by their mothers and other family members.

In the United States, the number of underclass least advantaged continues to grow. In 1991, 22.2 percent of American children under 16 years of age were living in poverty, in comparison to 16 percent of children under 18 years of age who were living in poverty in 1979.[56] Kozol (1990: p. 52) estimates that there are approximately 500,000 homeless children, whose average age is 6. He reports the condition of these homeless children:

> Whooping cough and tuberculosis, once regarded as archaic illnesses, are now familiar in the shelters. Shocking numbers of these children have not been inoculated and for this reason cannot go to school. Those who do are likely to be two years behind grade level. Many get to class so tired and hungry they cannot concentrate. Others are ashamed to go to school because of shunning by their peers. Classmates label them "the hotel children" and don't want to sit beside them. Even their teachers sometimes keep their distance . . . . Often unable to bathe, they bring the smell of destitution with them into school. There *is* a smell of destitution, I may add. It is the smell of sweat and filth and urine. Like many journalists, I often find myself ashamed to be resisting the affection of a tiny child whose entire being seems to emanate pathology. So, in a terrifying sense, these children have become American untouchables. (Kozol, 1990: p. 52)

Homeless children have also been found to suffer from depression, developmental delays, behavioral problems, and educational underachievement (Goins & Cesarone, 1993; Rafferty & Shinn, 1991).

Eighty percent of the children eligible for Head Start do not get this help (Kozol, 1990: p. 52). Furthermore, only 21 percent of 3- and 4-year-old children from families with incomes below $20,000 were found to attend day care, in comparison to 51 percent of children from families of income above $34,000 (Dorrell, 1992). The richest nation in the world is twentieth in infant mortality, which reflects the fact that the poorest families, 20 percent of the U. S. population, receive only 4.6 percent of the national family income.[57] In a 28-month survey, 4.7 million youth were found to have no health insurance and another 28 million to have insurance for only a portion of that time period.[58]

In his inaugural speech as mayor of New York, David Dinkins (1990) stressed the obligation to help least advantaged children:

> We must start with the most vulnerable and the most precious of all our people, our children. As we join together here in this pageant of progress and democracy, there is, this morning, somewhere in this city, a child born addicted to crack, a child suffering from AIDS, a child beaten down by the deprivation of poverty, a child abandoned, a child forgotten, a child whose dream has already been denied. No matter how rich and powerful we become, we cannot be satisfied when so many children experience the sunset of opportunity at the very dawn of their existence. (Dinkins, 1990: p. B-2)

ECLIPSE OF THE NUCLEAR FAMILY

The nuclear family is being pulverized. Between 1970 and 1992, the percentage of children raised in one-parent homes more than doubled.[59] More and more teenagers and other single women are having children out of wedlock. Single women accounted for 26.6 percent of all births in 1990, in comparison to 5.3 percent in 1960.[60] Between 1985 and 1990, the percentage of births to single women under 18 years of age increased by 16 percent (*Kids Count*, 1993: p. 32). The 360,645 babies born to women under 20 in 1990 represent almost 9 percent of all births for that year (*Kids Count*, 1993: p. 32).

Divorce and single parenthood have crippling effects. Seventy-five percent of children of single parents under 30 years of age live in poverty (*The Unfinished Agenda*, 1991: p. 2.). Children in single-parent homes are more than five times more likely to be poor in comparison to children in two-parent homes (Davis & McCaul, 1991: p. 52). Children were also reported to represent the fastest-growing poverty group. Forty percent of all poor people in America are children, and the younger the children, the greater are their chances of living in poverty (Dorrell, 1992). Poverty was found to be the most common predictor for at-risk youth. Poor children often arrive at school inadequately clothed and nourished and lacking proper medical care. They have problems with self-esteem resulting in part from parents who are themselves high school dropouts and failures (Dorrell, 1992). Eighty percent of the fathers and 70 percent of the mothers of high school dropouts were dropouts themselves (Dorrell, 1992: p. 9). Children in poverty are at greater risk of having discipline problems, of being suspended, and of being discouraged from pursuing their education (*Dealing with Dropouts*, 1987; Dorrell, 1992). They are also at greater risk for health problems, such as infant mortality, delayed intellectual development in infancy and preschool years, and poor academic performance in school leading to failure and dropout (Huston, 1989).

Children from one-parent families were found to be academically frustrated. They tend to drop out of school, and repeat the poverty cycle (Dorrell, 1992; McCormick, 1989; *The Unfinished Agenda*, 1991). They are at greater risk of being runaways, drug abusers, dropouts, truants, low academic achievers, and victims of violent crime and sexual abuse (Ellenwood, Majsterek, & Jones, 1991; Galston, 1993; Hoyle, 1993; *Kids Count*, 1993; Margolin, 1992; Powers, Eckenrode, & Jaklitsch, 1990; McCormick, 1989; Schloesser, 1992). By comparison to children in two-parent families, they were found to have lower performance on standardized tests (Natriello, McDill, & Pallas, 1990), to receive lower grades in school (Milne, Myers, Rosenthal, & Ginsberg, 1986), and to be almost twice as likely to drop out of school (Huston, 1989; Stedman, Salganik, & Celebuski, 1988). Daughters from mother-only families are also more likely to have adolescent pregnancies and low earnings in adulthood (Huston, 1989).

One out of three female-headed households is started by a teen mother (*Kids Count*, 1993: p. 32). Their children are more likely to have developmental delays and behavioral problems and to become academic failures and delinquents (*Kids Count*, 1993: p. 32). Furthermore, children born to teenage mothers often grow up to be teenage parents themselves (McCormick, 1989).

Sixteen percent of all children in 1990 in the United States lived with a stepparent.[61] Estimates of the percentage of children who will live with a stepparent before they are 18 years of age range from 33 to 60 percent (Wingert & Kantrowitz: 1990). Unfortunately, stepparenthood does not recreate the nuclear family. Stepchildren are more likely than children in two-parent homes to be lower in reading ability, to lack of impulse control, and to have diminished self-esteem (Amato & Ochiltree, 1987). Stepchildren were found to display more antisocial behavior (Wadsworth, Burnell, Taylor, & Butler, 1985). They were also found to experience lessened closeness with their natural parent and increased resentment, guilt, fear, despair, and disciplinary problems (Webber, 1988).[62] Stepchildren often suffer from problems of self-esteem and regress to earlier developmental stages (Phillips, 1986). Finally, the presence of stepfathers has been found significantly associated with greater chance of sexual abuse (Finkelhor, 1993; *Healthy Children*: 1988; Sariola & Uutela, 1992).

The skipgeneration, kids raised by their grandparents because of drug and alcohol addictions of the parents, often do poorly in school, defy authority, and have problems making friends. They exhibit physical aggressiveness and feelings of isolation, abandonment, and rejection from their parents (Seligmann, 1990: p. 46). Rat-pack youth, teenage pregnancy, teenage drug pushers, skinheads, head-bangers,[63] symptoms of the disintegration of the nuclear family, have become threats to America's future.

The traditional role of the mother in the two-parent home as caretaker and educator has been relegated to a variety of child-care alternatives. From 1975 to 1992, the percentage of employed wives with husbands present and with a child 1 year of age and under has increased by 84.1 percent, namely from 30.8 percent to 56.7 percent.[64] Similarly, from 1975 to 1992, the percentage of employed wives with husbands present with a child under 6 years of age has increased by 63.2 percent, that is, from 36.7 to 59.9 percent.[65] As a result, children are raised in a variety of day-care arrangements riddled by fundamental problems such as high staff turnover. From 1977 to 1988, staff turnover in child-care centers almost tripled, from 15 to 41 percent, while the average replacement rate for all other occupations was 19.4 percent (Galinsky, 1990c; National Association for the Education of Young Children, 1985; Whitebook, Howes, Phillips, & Pemberton, 1989). Some of the major causes of staff turnover are low pay, lack of benefits, and stressful working conditions (Kagan, 1990; Whitebook, Howes, Phillips, & Pemberton, 1989).

DAY CARE FOR INFANTS: DILEMMA OR DISASTER?

Standards for quality day care for infants are found lacking, which makes it difficult, if not impossible, to determine the quality of day-care centers. Meryl Frank (1990), a child-care expert, reports her feelings after visiting a day-care center recommended for her child: "I saw this line of cribs and all these babies with their arms out crying, wanting to be picked up. I felt like crying myself" (quoted in Wingert & Kantrowitz, 1990: p. 86). She adds that no matter how good the day-care center is supposed to be, "there's the disturbing question that lurks in the back of every working parent's mind:

what is this doing to my kids?" (quoted in Wingert & Kantrowitz, 1990: p. 86).

The greatest uncertainty concerns infants who are put in nursery care during the first year of life, especially if they enter day care during the time their first attachment is forming. Between 6 and 12 months of age, infants form specific attachments to their mothers and fathers, whom they prefer to any other person. Infants, at this age, center their activities around their parents and look for them when they are in distress, frightened, or sick. This behavior typically lasts until 24 months of age. Infants need to feel securely attached in order to develop a set of expectations about their social world and about themselves as worthy of care. However, being left in day care for most of the day may be interpreted by them as rejection and make them feel unwanted or unwantable (Bowlby, 1965).

Depending on the parents' promptness of response to their signals, infants will develop secure, insecure avoidant, or insecure ambivalent attachment (Ainsworth, Blehar, Waters, & Walls, 1978). This classification allows for the prediction of a wide range of behaviors in toddlerhood and during school years. By comparison to the insecurely attached, securely attached children are expected to be more sociable, more positive in their behavior toward others, and less aggressive. They exhibit fewer temper tantrums and show more empathy and altruistic behavior. They are also expected to be more mature, independent, and well-behaved at school, as well as to exhibit greater self-esteem and self-cognition, and to be more resourceful. Finally, they have longer attention span in free play and are better at problem solving.

In light of the importance secure attachment has on personal and social development, the question is whether infants could develop securely when they are separated from their parents for most of the day. Belsky's (1988)[66] research findings indicate that infants less than 1 year old receiving 20 or more hours a week of nonmaternal care were at greater risk of developing insecure avoidant attachments. Forty-three percent of the children whose mothers worked at least 20 hours a week were found to be insecurely attached, as opposed to the 25 percent of insecurely attached infants whose mothers worked less than 20 hours a week (Belsky, 1988). These children were more likely to exhibit heightened aggression and noncompliance in preschool and early school years. Infants in full-time group care were also found to be more aggressive and hyperactive (Schwarz, Strickland, & Krolick, 1974) and more likely to be loners and to act out (Barton & Schwartz, 1981). Finally, infants spending more than 30 hours per week in day care were found to have poorer peer relationships and work habits and to be more difficult to discipline than those in part-time child care or exclusive maternal care (Wingert & Kantrowitz, 1990). Disturbance in the mother-infant relationship may thus interfere with the tasks of limit setting and self-control in toddlerhood.

Early full-time day care may also affect the quality of attachment by reducing infants' confidence in the availability and responsiveness of care, and especially in their sense of effectiveness in eliciting care. The consequence of improper emerging mother-infant bond warrants serious concern. Sroufe (1988) thus states:

> Secure attachment is not something inherent in the infant; it is a product of the infant caregiver interactive history. Infants who by the end of the first year are securely attached have experienced consistently responsive care. They have been picked up when seeking contact, comforted when distressed, and engaged with sensitively. Their gestures have been imbued with meaning, and they have been empowered by a responsive social environment. The securely attached infant has come to expect such emotional availability and responsiveness from the social world. (p. 285)

Research also suggests that working mothers may not be sufficiently sensitive to their infants' needs. Harried from the obligations of work, they may provide less direct attention to their children upon their return because of the various chores around the house and less "quality time" due to the stress they are constantly experiencing (Wingert & Kantrowitz, 1990). Similarly, stress in a one-parent home or dysfunctional marriage may reduce the effectiveness of the mother as sensitive caregiver. And while poor parents may be unable to afford better day care for their children, middle-class or wealthy parents consumed in their professions may be unwilling to invest sufficient time or effort to find quality day care. Hofferth (1989), in an article titled "Mothers versus Children: The Real Child Care Debate," argues that infant day care, which may benefit mothers, is intrinsically against the welfare of infants.

The over $20 billion yearly child-care industry that has sprung up in community organizations and rented car showrooms has not addressed the problem of providing alternative child rearing. The lack of quality day care and the effects of unsatisfactory care on children's development may no longer be ignored. Thompson (1988) expresses concern for the consequences that may result from the government's unwillingness to regulate and subsidize quality day care, and poor people's inability to afford such care:

> I am especially concerned with infants from lower-income families (including welfare recipients) because of the combined effects of socioeconomic stress, family characteristics, and low quality care that may be seriously problematic for the sociopersonality development of infants in the early years. (p. 280)

Fein and Fox (1988) argue:

> The issue of infant day care will not disappear and will indeed grow as
> women continue to enter the work force or return to their professions
> soon after childbirth. Second, all would agree that we have an obligation
> as a society to make high quality substitute care available to all families.
> (pp. 232–233)

Sroufe (1988) has also been cautious about the prospects of full-time
nonmaternal care for infants under 1 year. However, he did not claim that
infants in day-care centers are necessarily at greater risk than infants taken
care of at home. Essential ingredients for infants' positive experience in day
care are meeting infants' expectations concerning the availability of others
and enhancing infants' effectiveness in influencing their environment and in
eliciting prompt responding. Selecting quality day care also means having
stable arrangements and personal support to enable ongoing emotional
closeness:

> It seems doubtful that early, full-time day care would inevitably have
> negative consequences . . . . Should the infant have repeated experiences
> over time that separations are predictable and predictably terminated, that
> caregivers are emotionally available, and that they are accepting of the
> infants' ambivalence and remain emotionally close despite any distancing
> efforts on the part of the infant, one would expect a positive outcome
> ultimately. (Sroufe, 1988: p. 288)

Early studies of infant day care were usually conducted within the
framework of experimental university programs designed to examine the
impact of optimal early childhood day care on the development of high-risk
disadvantaged children. These university sponsored day-care centers had
low caregiver-infant ratios, systematic curricula, and responsive and sensitive
caregivers. When compared to a control group of high-risk disadvantaged
infants without such day-care experience, infants in these studies vocalized
more, were more interactive with their mother, and were more socially
competent during developmental tests at 24 months, and continued to be so
for the next several years (Ramey, Dorval, & Baker-Ward, 1983; Ramey &
Finkelstein, 1978). Enrollment in such high-quality day care did seem to
prevent the usual decline in IQ scores experienced by high-risk economically
disadvantaged children (Golden & Birns, 1983; Ramey & Campbell, 1977).
It also seemed to reinforce the association between infant-mother attachment
and mother's involvement and warmth toward her infant during the first year
of life (Burchinal, Bryant, Lee, & Ramey, 1992.)

NEW PATHS FROM KIBBUTZ NURSERIES

The nuclear family can no longer function without proper supports. There needs to be a congruence between work, family, and community so that mother and child do not doubt their relationship. Employment should not put mother and child in a strange situation.

Kibbutz infants spend most of their waking hours (7 A.M. to 3 P.M.) at the infant's house. In spite of being away from their parents, they have room to roam and grow into mature, autonomous, and healthy individuals. The kibbutz ecology of maternal employment has produced quality day care, mothers' availability, and stability of caregivers. Can we Americans learn from the kibbutz communal childcare system, which may be characterized in Buber's terms as an experiment that did not fail? Some guidelines for change are proposed below.

As in the kibbutz, mothers could share their primary caregiving role with mother substitutes in such a way that they would complement each other. Continuous and stable support from these caregivers would help the child grow.

Another suggested improvement is to relocate nurseries and day-care centers at parents' work site. By rapproaching parents and children, parents would no longer feel that they are dumping their children, and infants would no longer feel dumped in a strange environment. Parents would come to feed their newborns or simply feel free to drop by anytime during a break for a few minutes. They could also come to the day-care center to have their lunch with their children. Some pioneer companies in the United States have started to establish day-care centers close to the parents' place of work, thus allowing infants and parents to be close to each other (Whitaker, 1989).

This relocation could allow day-care workers to help toddlers solve the mystery of where mommy and daddy are during the day. Toddlers would visit their parents' workplace. They would be shown the work site, and what their parents do there would be explained to them. Parents' workplace, their job, and co-workers would become familiar to children. Back at the nursery, children would be given tools such as paper, pencils, scissors, needles, word processors, computers, or any other instruments that would help them learn more about their parents' occupations. Reciprocally, parents would get more involved in the daily activity of their children by volunteering their services and presence a couple of hours every month. They would provide a helping hand to set up the playground or new equipment or help with holiday preparations. Parents would also be invited to "show and tell" to present their professions or talents, or simply to introduce other siblings in the family. Dentists, for example, would bring their toothbrushes, carpenters their hammers and nails, and musicians their guitars or accordions. Parents who enjoy art could bring their paintbrushes, and mothers could show their newborn babies. This rapprochement would allow children to feel their parents' presence. And when their parents left the nursery, youngsters would know that they were present somewhere in the building. Children could now reason, "If I need mommy, she will come. I know where she is."

The child-care worker-child relationship is another important, if not the most important ingredient, of quality day care. Caregivers must be responsive, and provide a warm and positive environment to the child. They would encourage independence, autonomy, and nurturant control (Galinsky, 1990b). They would let children know that they are valued, trusted, and respected. The atmosphere they create should provide children with the feeling that they are living in a friendly world. Quality day care would establish appropriate methods for screening out insensitive day-care workers or mother substitutes who are unable to become attuned to children. Typically, insensitive caregivers do not answer children's signals appropriately, or they ignore them completely. They are indifferent to children's needs and psychologically unavailable or rejecting. Only such caring and responsive day-care workers could provide children from abusive or violent homes with a corrective emotional experience. By being physically and emotionally available, day-care workers would give these children the love, respect, and security needed to form new attachments and trust. Through these significant relationships, children from violent homes would break the circle of violence and find alternative ways of relating to themselves, to others, and to the world.

Supervised placement in licensed day-care centers as well as periodic on-the-job training would allow child-care workers initially judged responsive to develop an authoritative style of child rearing. They will learn to be warm and friendly and to respond enthusiastically and with empathy to children. They will learn to use reason and logic while providing children with explanations to help them develop self-control and cooperation (Galinsky, 1990a). While applying clear and consistent rules, they will not be afraid to place high expectations on children and will want children to be independent and helpful. Openness of communication and nondirectiveness would go in both directions. Children raised in this mode reach optimum development and high self-esteem. They become more independent and have greater confidence in themselves and in others.

The other two styles of child rearing are the permissive and the authoritarian styles. Individuals who adopt a permissive style are warm and communicative, but incapable of imposing any demand for maturity and control. By contrast, those who adopt an authoritarian style impose on children high expectations for maturity and control, but prevent the establishment of a warm atmosphere or true communication with the child (Baumrind, 1971). In Stone's study (1991), 14 out of 30 caregivers working in the 17 day-care centers examined were found to use restrictive language. Such a language, characteristic of authoritarian caregivers, was found to induce aggression and social incompetence in children (Bagley, 1989; Farran, 1982; Hartup, 1970, Hesov & Berger, 1978; Marshner, 1988; Stone, 1993; Turiel, 1986; Woolfolk, 1990).

As in the kibbutz, mutual help and cooperation would be the norms. Small groups of children would be formed. Educators would encourage cooperation by rewarding group performance and by initiating group games. Children would be rewarded for relying on each other for comfort and support rather than for competing to gain the caregiver's attention. Amount of personal contact, richness of verbal stimulation, cleanliness and colorfulness of the building and classroom, as well as caregivers' knowledge of child development are also important.

One issue educators often grapple with in their formulation of quality day care is the proper mix of structure and gross versus fine motor skill activities. Children require diverse experiences and ample opportunity for physical, social, and verbal interaction. They need an environment to express and develop their native curiosity through play, exploration, and fantasy as well as through more structured activities. However, too much external structure guidance or stress diminishes their sense of autonomy and self-efficacy (Sigel, 1987). The present trend toward increased screening, fine motor skill development, and testing beginning in full-time kindergarten or even preschool is often misguided and, in general, reduces rather than enhances motivation, individual problem-solving ability, and moral development.

Preschools and kindergartens should not be placed in preacademia. Even the best-intended child-care programs that attempt to teach reading, writing, and arithmetic to 3- and 4-year-old children could be harmful:

> Children subjected to formal teaching at such early ages tended to be less creative when they entered school, registered more anxiety about tests and soon lost the academic advantage with which they started elementary school. (Hechinger, 1989: p. B–11)

As in the kibbutz, children would have room to roam and explore freely. They would be given back their medium of expression—play. During unstructured times, children are very busy making a tea party or dressing up as princesses or nurses. They feed their dolls, dress them, or comb their hair and bathe them. They are train conductors or pilots flying their airplanes. They are busy playing. Play is not an empty activity. It provides the building blocks for children's cognitive development. The different kinds of play children engage in were found to follow stages (Rubin, Fein, & Vandenberg, 1983). Through play, children learn how things feel and look. Through role-playing and pretending they experience how it is to be someone else. The conflicts and disagreements children experience while playing with other children stimulate their social skills and make them understand that there are other perspectives besides their own (Bearison, Magzamen, & Filardo, 1986) and other ways of relating to the world. Play also provides avenues for children from abusive or violent homes to express their feelings. The violence and anger they experience could be rechanneled against toys and stuffed animals (Wallach, 1993). Dramatic play could help these children gain control over traumatic experiences by repeating them over and over again. Painting, drawing, story telling, and story sharing are other means through which children can communicate their emotions.

Day-care centers could become the heart of the community. Activities such as parties, picnics, and shows performed by children would strengthen children's and parents' bonds to the community and eventually reduce anxiety and feelings of estrangement by enhancing a sense of growing up in a community of caring adults.[67]

The resources of the best day-care centers and nurseries would be made available to all children as a result of government stipends. Afternoon programs would stimulate the intellectual, emotional, and social development of underprivileged preschoolers and kindergartners. In conformity with the fair equality of opportunity principle, private day care would become public, that is, open to all.

NEW PATHS FROM THE YOUTH SOCIETY

Nursery care clearly is not the only problem of America's educational abyss. Apathy, cutthroat competition, aggression, drugs, and delinquency are some of the problems educators face daily in primary, middle, and high schools. Adopting the model of the Youth Society, the emphasis would be on group dynamics. The pressure to compete would yield to a cooperative atmosphere. Egalitarian peer groups, autonomous in decisionmaking, would participate in community work and vocational training. High schools in Hanover, New Hampshire; Brookline, Massachusetts; Bronx, New York (Wasserman, 1976), and more recently in Reading, Massachusetts, (Murphy, 1988) have implemented Kohlberg's model of the Just Community, which attempts to reproduce the dynamics of the Youth Society in the United States. In addition to regular curricula, visits to community organizations such as Alcoholic Anonymous, prisons, and churches were required of the participants. Despite ups and downs, these schools have been effective in teaching self-discipline, responsibility, and empathy.

In conformity with the difference principle, vocational skills should be as valued as academic ones so that the academically least advantaged could gain self-worth and esteem by engaging in other valued enterprises. They would learn through on-the-job training in prominent community businesses how to be skilled technicians, for example, in refrigeration or television repair, and they would carry out their tasks proudly. Even day-care centers could provide rich and meaningful work experiences to high school students spending some of their after-school hours working with young children.

In conclusion, the kibbutz educational system offers new perspectives in education that could provide borderline delinquents, underprivileged, and underdogs a fighting chance for developing their cognitive and moral capacities.

POSTSCRIPT

Many Americans wonder why our society continues to decay. To find an answer, we must focus on anomic youth. The problems of our youth emerge in a society in which the family is no longer properly functioning. The theoretical underpinnings of Rawls combined with the empirical data found on the kibbutz, offer a sound approach for attacking our growing anomie. For those who have not lost hope in strengthening the family and re-creating their communities, this book opens new avenues to meet this challenge.

Appendix A

U.N. Declaration of the Rights of the Child

Principle 2: The child shall enjoy special protection and shall be given opportunities and facilities, by law, and by other means, to enable him to develop physically, mentally, spiritually and socially in a healthy and normal manner and in conditions of freedom and dignity. In the enactment of laws for this purpose, the best interest of the child shall be the paramount consideration.

Principle 6: The child, for the full and harmonious development of his personality, needs love and understanding.

Principle 7: The child is entitled to receive an education, which shall be free and compulsory, at least in the elementary stages. He shall be given an education which will promote his general culture, and enable him, on a basis of equal opportunity, to develop his abilities his individual judgement, and his sense of moral and social responsibility, and to become a useful member of society.

Principle 9: The child shall be protected against all forms of neglect, cruelty, and exploitation. He shall not be the subject of traffic in any form.

Source: (United Nations, General Assembly Resolution 1386 [XIV] adopted Nov. 20, 1959, and published 1960, *Official Records of the General Assembly, 14th Session, Supplement no. 16*, p. 20).

Appendix B

Self-Report Research Instrument

DISSATISFACTION WITH OFFICIAL DATA

Modern researchers on delinquency have adopted self-report as their primary research tool because of the following objections to official data:

1. Official records are based on misrepresentative samples and thus provide a distorted picture of the distribution of criminal behavior (Schur, 1973; Sellin & Wolfgang, 1964).

2. An unknown number of offenses are never discovered, and those discovered are never reported to the authorities (Hirschi, 1969)

3. A good deal of important information, such as circumstances of the offense and victim-offender relationship, are rarely recorded (Hindelang, Hirschi, & Weis, 1981).

4. Official data suffer from practical limitations since there is no way to refine official data statistics to compensate for undiscovered and unreported crimes.

STRENGTH OF SELF-REPORT

The proponents of self-report aim at constructing a measure of delinquency identical to that explicit in the official definition and implicit in the official procedure, but without the omissions, mistakes, and bias found in official measures.

An essential argument in favor of self-report is based on the dictum, "If you want to know something about a person, ask that person directly." The most reliable source of information is assumed to be the person with direct knowledge of the events experienced. People committing delinquent acts are, furthermore, assumed to be aware of their actions and, therefore, capable of recalling and reporting them.

Short and Nye's (1958) pioneer study has helped establish self-report as a legitimate method of measuring delinquency. On the basis of the questionnaire they administered in schools and institutions, Short and Nye have shown that adolescents are willing and perfectly able to report behavior on taboo subjects and delinquency. Furthermore, they found that these reports were internally consistent.

RELIABILITY OF SELF-REPORT

Reliability of self-report questionnaire items has been established by several studies using test-retest reliability or coefficient of stability with time gaps between administrations ranging from hours to several years. To be sure, the test-retest reliability of self-report depends on the interval between administrations of the test and retest. When this interval is short, the reliability coefficients obtained are generally very high. Kulik, Stein, and Sarbin (1968a) obtained a .98 coefficient of reliability for a 51-item checklist when time between test and retest ranged from 90 to 120 minutes. The split-half reliability of the total was also high (.96). Dentler and Monroe (1961), who retested their subjects ($\underline{N}$ = 111) two weeks later, found that the adolescent theft scale "was responded to identically on test and retest by between 92 to 100 percent of the subjects" (p. 735). These studies thus show impressive evidence of short-term stability of self-report results.

Farrington (1973) criticized those high coefficients by arguing that these may be inflated because subjects may remember their prior responses as a consequence of the short interval between test and retest. He therefore planned and conducted a test-retest with a two-year interval. He nonetheless obtained a correlation gamma of .62 with $\underline{N}$ = 393 on a self-report questionnaire that included 38 items, confirming the reliability of self-report data.

VALIDITY OF SELF-REPORT

Validity of self-report data was established by a large-scale self-report study conducted by Hindelang, Hirschi, and Weis (1981) in Seattle, Washington, during the 1978–1979 academic year. Respondents from three populations were sampled. The first included official nondelinquents, that is, high school students enrolled in public school for the 1977–1978 academic year who had no official record of delinquent behavior. The second sample was composed of borderline official delinquents, that is, adolescents with a record of contact with the Seattle police, but with no record in juvenile court. The third sample was drawn from the population of official delinquents, who were adolescents referred to the King County Division of Youth Services—the juvenile court serving Seattle. Within these strata, subjects were further stratified by race, sex, and median income of census tract to form the eighteen subject pools required of the design.

The basic self-report instrument contained sixty-nine items grouped into five categories: contact with the criminal justice system, serious crimes, general delinquency, drug offenses, and school and family offenses. The adoption of a definition of delinquency identical to that explicit in legal codes and implicit in the juvenile justice system allowed for the correlation of a variety of official measures with self-reported measures of delinquency. Self-report of police contacts were alternative indicators of self-reported acts of official delinquency.

Questions about delinquent behavior that did not mention any specific time but that started with "Have you ever" or "Did you ever," as in "Have you ever been picked up by the police?" produced the strongest correlation with other variables. For example, the eight indices—amorality, parental supervision, achievement orientation, respect for teacher, respect for parents, respect for the police, respect for friends, and being picked up by the police—produced a multiple R of .72. among white males. Questions of the "ever" variety were also found to be the best predictors of self-reported official behavior. For example, in response to the question, "Have you ever been referred to court by the police?" 95 percent of those reporting no record had in fact no such record with local police. The gamma for self-report of official contact and official indicators of such contact was high, ranging between .63 to .83 among males and .51 to .85 among females. Moderate to low correlations were also obtained between unofficial sources such as informant report of delinquency and official record of it: .32 to .42 for males and .32 to .42 for females (Elliot & Voss, 1974; Hindelang, Hirschi, & Weis, 1981; Hirschi, 1969).

METHOD OF ADMINISTRATION

Four methods of administration were tested by the Seattle study: anonymous versus nonanonymous questionnaire and anonymous versus nonanonymous interview. It was expected that the anonymous questionnaire in which the subject's identity was concealed would allow the youths to reveal sensitive information.

On the basis of test-retests of twenty-two self-report items, official delinquency records, and informer methods, anonymous conditions were not found superior to nonanonymous ones. Although fluctuations across methods were noted, there was no consistency superior performance of any one method. Reliability coefficients and internal consistency measures were as high for questionnaires as for interviews, and for anonymous as for nonanonymous conditions and, therefore, were unaffected by the particular method used to collect the data.

The Seattle study thus establishes self-report as a reliable and valid research instrument of great value within the appropriate population, that is, of white students in school who are not seriously delinquent.

Appendix C

Questionnaire

Please check or fill in the answer

Sex (a) Male (b) female.

How old are you?

Do you agree with the following statements? Please check one of the answers.

1. Most people do not care about what happens to you. (a) Agree (b) Undecided (c) Disagree.

2. Young people are always getting into trouble. (a) Agree (b) Undecided (c) Disagree.

3. There are not enough places for children to play. (a) Agree (b) Undecided (c) Disagree.

4. A lot of men in the neighborhood do not have work. (a) Agree (b) Undecided (c) Disagree.

5. Most of the families in the neighborhood know each other. (a) Agree (b) Undecided (c) Disagree.

6. Most of the people around here do not care about what happens to you. (a) Agree (b) Undecided (c) Disagree.

Please check one of the answers.

7. How does your family compare with other families in the neighborhood? (a) Agree (b) Undecided (c) Disagree.

8. How do you personally like your neighborhood as a place to live? (a) Agree (b) Undecided (c) Disagree.

Do you agree with the following statements? Please check one of the answers.

9. Everyone in the world is out for himself? (a) Agree (b) Undecided (c) Disagree.

10. It is hard for young people without a high school diploma to find a job. (a) Agree (b) Undecided (c) Disagree.

11. The community should take care of those who cannot take care of themselves. (a) Agree (b) Undecided (c) Disagree.

Please check one of the answers.

12. Does your father know where you are when you are away from home? (a) Often (b) Sometimes (c) Never.

13. Does your mother know where you are when you are away from home? (a) Often (b) Sometimes (c) Never.

14. Do your friends know where you are when you are away from home? (a) Often (b) Sometimes (c) Never.

15. When you come across things you do not understand, does your father help you with them? (a) Often (b) Sometimes (c) Never.

16. When you come across things you do not understand, does your mother help you with them? (a) Often (b) Sometimes (c) Never.

17. When you come across things you do not understand, do your friends help you with them? (a) Often (b) Sometimes (c) Never.

18. Do you share your feelings and thoughts with your father? (a) Often (b) Sometimes (c) Never.

19. Do you share your feelings and thoughts with your mother? (a) Often (b) Sometimes (c) Never.

20. Do you share your feelings and thoughts with your friends? (a) Often (b) Sometimes (c) Never.

21. Do you talk to your father about your future plans? (a) Often (b) Sometimes (c) Never.

22. Do you talk to your mother about your future plans? (a) Often (b) Sometimes (c) Never.

23. Do you talk to your friends about your future plans? (a) Often (b) Sometimes (c) Never.

24. Did you ever feel unwanted by your father? (a) Often (b) Sometimes (c) Never.

25. Did you ever feel unwanted by your mother? (a) Often (b) Sometimes (c) Never.

26. Did you ever feel unwanted by your friends? (a) Often (b) Sometimes (c) Never.

27. Would you like to be the kind of person your mother is? (a) In most ways (b) In some ways (c) Not at all.

28. Would you like to be the kind of person your father is? (a) In most ways (b) In some ways (c) Not at all.

29. Would you like to be the kind of persons your friends are? (a) In most ways (b) In some ways (c) Not at all.

30. Would your father stick by you if you got into bad trouble? (a) Certainly (b) Probably (c) No.

31. Would your mother stick by you if you got into bad trouble? (a) Certainly (b) Probably (c) No.

32. Would your friends stick by you if you got into bad trouble? (a) Certainly (b) Probably (c) No.

33. Do you ever feel that there is nothing to do? (a) Agree (b) Undecided (c) Disagree.

34. Have you ever taken little things worth less than five dollars that did not belong to you? (a) Never (b) More than a year ago (c) During the last year or more than a year ago.

35. Have you ever taken things of some value worth between five and fifty dollars that did not belong to you? (a) Never (b) More than a year ago (c) During the last year or more than a year ago.

36. Have you ever taken things of large value worth more than fifty dollars that did not belong to you? (a) Never (b) More than a year ago (c) During the last year or more than a year ago.

37. Have you ever taken a car for a ride without its owner's permission? (a) Never (b) More than a year ago (c) During the last year or more than a year ago.

38. Have you ever taken a tractor for a ride without its owner's permission? (a) Never (b) More than a year ago (c) During the last year or more than a year ago.

39. Have you ever taken a bike for a ride without its owner's permission? (a) Never (b) More than a year ago (c) During the last year or more than a year ago.

40. Whenever you take something that does not belong to you, do you give it back? (a) Always (b) Sometimes (c) Never.

41. How important is getting good grades to you personally? (a) Very important (b) Important (c) Not important.

42. How important do you think good grades are for getting the kind of job you want when you finish school? (a) Very important (b) Important (c) Not important.

43. What is the worst thing about getting caught for stealing? (a) The police might not treat you well (b) Your parents would be angry (c) Your friends would look down on you (d) Do not know (e) Other adults in the community would make fun of you.

Do you agree with the following statements? Please check one of the answers.

44. To get ahead one has to do things that are not right. (a) Agree (b) Undecided (c) Disagree.

45. People who break the law are almost always caught and punished. (a) Agree (b) Undecided (c) Disagree.

46. Most of the things people call delinquency do not hurt anyone. (a) Agree (b) Undecided (c) Disagree.

47. It is alright to get around the law if you can get away with it. (a) Agree (b) Undecided (c) Disagree.

48. Suckers deserve to be taken advantage of. (a) Agree (b) Undecided (c) Disagree.

49. Most of the criminals should not be blamed for the things they have done. (a) Agree (b) Undecided (c) Disagree.

Please check one of the answers.

50. Do you respect your best friends' opinions about the important things in life? (a) Agree (b) Undecided (c) Disagree.

51. Who do you spend most of your free time with? (a) Friends (b) Family (c) Other adults.

52. Most of the people can be trusted. (a) Agree (b) Undecided (c) Disagree.

53. Do you work? (a) Yes (b) No.

54. Getting a good education is harder than getting a good job. (a) Agree (b) Undecided (c) Disagree.

Notes

1. *Chach-chach(im)* refers to a manner of dressing and acting among lower-class macho males. They usually wear very tight pants, a partially unbuttoned shirt, a large gold chain around the neck, and shiny shoes with moderately high heels.

2. Throughout this chapter, the term "original position" will be used to refer to its first stage. The other three stages are examined in chapter 2.

3. Rawls' description of utilitarianism is based on Henry Sidgwick's (1907) perception of this theory. Sidgwick uses the phrase, "the total amounts of pleasure and pain that may be expected to result respectively from maintaining any given rule as at present established and from endeavoring to introduce that which is proposed in its stead" (1907: p. 477). This is one of three interrelated methods that provide the basis for Sidgwick's ethics. Schneewind (1967) also points out that utilitarianism is Sidgwick's dominant method.

4. Dworkin (1975: p. 49) supports the device of the veil of ignorance because it is related to the right of equal respect and guarantees that no one secures himself a better position because of particular talents and abilities.

5. It should be noted that a conservative attitude toward risk under uncertainty is a common assumption of decision theory, zero-sum game theory, and economics. Rawls (1971) perceives the bargaining model within the framework of the zero sum game theory.

6. Had this child been granted the same due process protections against loss of liberty as an adult, his commitment would have violated the equal protection clause of the Fourteenth Amendment. To emphasize the unequal status of children, one also notes that in *Vitek v. Jones*, 100 S. Ct., 1254 (1980), the Court decided that even prisoners in a maximum security facility have a sufficient "liberty interest" to be entitled to a fact-finding hearing before being transferred to a mental hospital (*Vitek v. Jones*, cited in Cohen, 1982: p. 73).

7. *Statistical Abstract of the United States 1922*, No. 45: p. 88; *Statistical Abstract of the United States 1993*, No. 113: p. 73.

8. *Statistical Abstract of the United States 1993*, No. 113: p. 400.

9. Ibid.

10. *Statistical Abstract of the United States 1991*, No. 111: p. 391.

11. *Statistical Abstract of the United States 1989*, No. 109: p. 172; *Statistical Abstract of the United States 1990*, No. 110: p. 176.

12. *Statistical Abstract of the United States 1993*, No. 113: p. 209.

13. *Judicial Training and Research for Child Custody Litigation*, 1992.

14. The words children and youth are used interchangeably to refer to minors, that is, to individuals who are less than 18 years of age.

15. Naagi (1977) indicated that the Center for the Prevention of Child Abuse reported that 80 percent of incarcerated criminals were abused by their parents when they were children. See also Flowers (1986) and Sroufe & Fleeson, 1986.

16. See also Eckenrode, Laird, and Doris, 1993.

17. Two to 7 million return to an empty home every day (Weisberg, 1988: p. 4). Siegel and Senna (1994) estimate that 7% of all children under 13 years of age are latchkey children. See also Whisler, 1991.

18. *Drug Abuse and Prevention Programs for Youth*, 1991.

19. *Statistical Abstract of the United States 1993*, No. 113: p. 208.

20. Ibid.; *Sourcebook of Criminal Justice Statistics 1975*: p. 554.

21. *Statistical Abstract of the United States 1992*, No. 112: p. 8.

22. Ibid.

23. Irwin (1970) examined a subgroup in adult prisons known as state-raised youth. These adult inmates "graduated" from juvenile institutions. They are known to form groupings that engage in predatory, violent, and homosexual behavior.

24. Many other Supreme Court decisions show that youngsters do not have the same legal status as adults and, therefore, do not enjoy the same constitutional protections of their liberty. For example, in *McKiever v. Pennsylvania*, 403 U.S. 528, 91 S. Ct. 1976 (1970), the Supreme Court upheld that juveniles are not entitled to a jury or public trial in delinquency proceedings. In *Ingraham v. Wright*, 430 U.S. 651, 97 S. Ct. 1401 (1977), the court held that due process does not require notice of hearing prior to the imposition of corporal punishment at school. In *New Jersey v. T.L.O.*, 469 U.S 325, 105 S. Ct. 733 (1985), the Supreme Court held that neither probable cause nor search warrant is necessary to search a student in high school. These actions, if taken against adults, would constitute violations of the Fourth, Sixth, and Fourteenth Amendments.

25. Gewirth (1978) also uses a proportionality principle to formulate the idea of gradual increase of the child's freedom. This principle states that with greater development of ability and reason, children should be allowed to participate in decisions affecting their lives. When these capacities are fully mature, they should be allowed to decide autonomously.

26. Coercion here means punishment by law and not merely the expression of moral disapproval.

27. Rawls (1971), nevertheless, claims that his model of justice is compatible with either capitalist or socialist economic systems.

28. See also Charvet (1969).

29. The kibbutz secretariat is composed of the treasurer, the secretary, the work allocator, and managers of the production and consumption branches. Its task is to coordinate between branches and to be responsible for the administration of the kibbutz.

30. As of 1982, the Takam (United Kibbutz Movement), which includes 164 kibbutzim, has been composed of two movements that for many years were separate: the Ehud and Meuhud. The kibbutz Artzi of Hashomer Hatzair, which includes 80 kibbutzim, has historically most zealously guarded kibbutz ideology and was slower, for instance, to adopt familial sleeping arrangements. Finally, the religious kibbutz movement Hadatti includes 14 kibbutzim (Near, 1982: p. 12). Since 1965, the Takam and Artzi movements have been politically united, with the goal of influencing governmental programs.

31. Research shows that kibbutzim have been successful in incorporating direct democracy into industrial shops (Leviatan, 1973; Rosner, 1980; Tannenbaum, 1980).

32. Sepharadic Jews originate from Arab countries and Mediterranean European countries, whereas Askenazi Jews originate from western, central, and eastern Europe.

33. Hindelang and his colleagues (1981) found that the subgroups black males and serious delinquents by official record, for whom truthful statements are not so flattering, were less likely to report offenses known to the police and less likely to report school failures. See also Elliot and Voss (1974) and Hirschi (1969).

34. Hirschi, leading proponent of self-report, tested and validated his questionnaire and theory on the basis of the research he conducted in Richmond, California in 1964. Richmond was then populated mainly by manual workers. Its black population was 12 percent (Hirschi, 1969). Hirschi administered his questionnaire to 5,545 out of 17,500 students who entered public junior and senior high school in the fall of 1964. Out of these 5,545 subjects, 4,077 answered the questionnaire in full.

35. Neither nuclear-family children from Tel Aviv nor those from a small farming community were selected since they would not have been representative of the population. A typical small suburban community 10 kilometers north of Haifa, and a somewhat larger than average kibbutz located in northern Galilee, with the typical economic and demographic makeup of other kibbutzim, were chosen.

36. Glueck and Glueck (1950) compared the family background of delinquents to that of nondelinquents of the same socioeconomic status and found that the parents of the delinquents were less concerned with their children's welfare. They did not care whether their children were getting into trouble and either had very vague or no plans for their children's future.

37. Hirschi (1969) offers the example of the businessman who would not dare cheat on his wife while working in the same town, but who easily indulges in such behavior while on business trips.

38. Hirschi also stresses the relation between harsh punishment and delinquency: "Some recent writers have reached the conclusion that the 'real' purpose of punishment is to generate that which it is ostensibly designed to prevent" (1969: p. 102, n. 35).

39. The suffering of these youth and the repercussions on society as a result of their dropping out are profound. For example, 82 percent of Americans in prison were found to be high school dropouts (*The Unfinished Agenda*, 1991: p. 11).

40. In Hirschi's (1969) sample, 90 percent of the students agreed with the statement "It is hard for young people without a high school diploma to find a job."

41. Kornhauser (1978) and Hirschi (1969) also note that in none of these orientations do illegal acts acquire the status of norms.

42. Anomie means normless. "Nomos" in Greek means law and "a" means a lack of. Therefore, anomie does not mean maladjusted. Maladjustment may be one consequence of being anomic, but not all maladjusted are anomic.

43. At this stage, the delinquent's calculations are purely tactical. They are rooted in situational factors and in social structure, not in culture. The ideology of the normless or anomic is a cognitive orientation that asserts the primacy of self-interest (Hirschi, 1969; Kornhauser, 1978).

44. The rate of teenage suicide has more than doubled in the United States from 1970 to 1987 (Davis & McCaul, 1991: p. 96), and has become the second leading cause of death for teenagers (Dorrell, 1992: p. 12).

45. Bettelheim spent seven weeks in the spring of 1964 in one Israeli kibbutz writing his book *The Children of the Dream*. One of the major criticisms of his participant observation was that he did not speak a word of Hebrew when he conducted his study.

46. A moshav is a community of small farmers who cooperatively own, maintain, and use certain equipment and property. Unlike the kibbutz, each family unit is a separate profit-making entity. Furthermore, the moshav does not have communal child-rearing practices.

47. Riesman, who condemns peer groups that do not tolerate variety or differences as "cutting down to size anyone who stands up or stands out in any direction" (1950: p. 71), recognizes that democratic peer groups could enhance autonomy.

48. Riesman (1950) and Flacks (1978) criticize nuclear-family parents' attempts to establish egalitarian relationships with their children. Their techniques of discipline, which have become more psychological, less authoritarian, and based on giving and withdrawing love, are subtle manipulations and rationalizations to which the child responds in kind. Green (1946) argues that the constant threat of love withdrawal expressed in such a statement as, "Eat your soup; otherwise I will not love you," is at the root of middle-class children's neurosis.

49. To develop his theory, Kohlberg (1971) interviewed for 20 years fifty males living in Chicago whose ages initially ranged between 10 and 16.

50. Children are placed at each corner of the Madsen Game Board and have to decide whether to cooperate or compete. The kibbutz ($n = 20$) and nuclear family ($n = 20$) children are placed initially in a cooperative reward structure. "They must move the pen through the four target circles in sequence to be rewarded. On the next series of trials, each child receives a reward only when the pen moves though his or her own designated target circle. Even when the instructions are changed in this way, cooperation is still the best strategy because, if the children pull against one another at cross-purposes, chances are that no one will receive many prizes" (Wrightsman, 1977: p. 287).

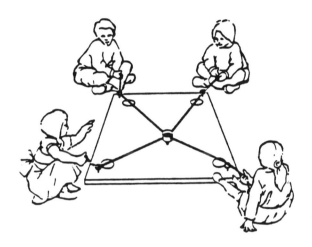

Source: *Social Psychology*, Second Edition, by Lawrence S. Wrightsman. Copyright © 1977 by Wadsworth, Inc. Reprinted by permission of Brooks/Cole Publishing Company, Pacific Grove, CA 93950.

51. In chapter 7, we shall examine the creation of Just Communities in the United States, which have adopted democratic decision-making procedures and values similar to those of the Youth Society.

52. *Statistical Abstract of Israel, 1989*, 1990: p. 166.

53. From 1976 to 1990, the rate rose from 3.2 to 16 per 10 thousand. From 1976 to 1986, the average age of victims of sexual abuse ranged from 7.1 to 7.7 years, and the modal age in 1991 was 2-5 years old (*Statistical Abstract of the United States 1990*, No. 110: p. 176; *Statistical Abstract of the United States 1993*, No. 113: p. 209).

54. A *Time* magazine article subtitled "A Rise in Brutal Crimes by the Young Shakes the Soul of Society" (Toufexis, 1989: pp. 52–58) describes some of the most brutal crimes commonly committed by youth. "Every 100 hours more youths die on the streets than were killed in the Persian Gulf" (Witkin et al., 1991: p. 26). See also Emery (1993).

55. *Statistical Abstract of the United States 1993*, No. 113: p. 93.

56. Ibid., p. 470; *Statistical Abstract of the United States 1987*, No. 107: p. 442.

57. Kozol, 1990: p. 51. See also Hobbs and Lippman, 1990.

58. *Statistical Abstract of the United States 1993*, No. 113: p. 115.

59. The percentage of children raised in one-parent homes rose from 12 percent in 1970 to 26 percent in 1992 (*Statistical Abstract of the United States 1993*, No. 113: p. 64).

60. *Statistical Abstract of the United States 1993*, No. 113: p. 77. *Statistical Abstract of the United States 1987*, No. 107: p. 61.

61. *Statistical Abstract of the United States 1993*, No. 113: p. 62.

62. See also Weisberg, 1988.

63. A precise definition of head-bangers eludes us. Interviews with head-bangers indicate that many like heavy metal music, devil worship, and witchcraft.

64. *Statistical Abstract of the United States 1993*, No. 113: p. 400.

65. Ibid.

66. Belsky's review generally involves interpretation of findings based on Ainsworth and colleagues' (1978) "Strange Situation" research method. The Strange Situation consists of the following eight episodes lasting 3 minutes each: (1) the mother brings the infant into a playroom and puts the infant down, (2) the infant is free to explore while the mother reads a magazine, (3) a stranger enters the room and tries to play with the infant, (4) the mother leaves the room, (5) the mother returns and the stranger leaves the room, (6) the mother leaves the infant alone in the room, (7) the stranger returns, and (8) the mother returns, greets, and picks up the infant. Assessment of the infant's attachment is based primarily on the infant's response to reunion with the mother, namely on episodes 5 and 8.

67. Research on social competence also stresses the long-term importance of emotional and motivational factors, development of positive self-image, and positive social relations with adults and peers (Zigler & Trickett, 1978).

Bibliography

Ainsworth, M. D. S., Blehar, M. C., Waters, E., & Walls, S. (1978). *Patterns of attachment: A psychological study of the Strange Situation.* Hillsdale, NJ: Erlbaum.

Ainsworth, M. D. S., & Wittig, B. A. (1969). Attachment and exploratory behavior of one-year olds in a Strange Situation. In B. M. Foss (Ed.), *Determinants of Infant Behavior* Vol. IV (pp. 111 136). London: Methuen.

Allen-Hagan, B., & Sickmund, M. (1993, July). Juveniles and violence: Juvenile offending and victimization. Washington, DC: Office of Justice and Delinquency Prevention, U.S. Department of Justice, Office of Justice Programs, 1–4.

Amato, P. R., & Ochiltree, G. (1987). Child and adolescent competence in intact, one-parent, and step-families. *Journal of Divorce*, *10*(10), 57–96.

Amir, Y. (1969). The effectiveness of the kibbutz-born soldier in the Israel Defense Forces. *Human Relations*, *22*(4), 333–344.

Aries, P. (1962). *Centuries of childhood: A social history of family life* (R. Baldick, Trans.). New York: Knopf.

Arthur, R., & Erickson, E. (1992). *Gangs and schools.* Holmes Beach, FL: Learning Publications. (ERIC Document Reproduction Service No. ED 358204)

Bachman, G., O'Malley, P., & Johnson, J. (1978). *Youth in transition, Vol. VI: Adolescence to adulthood: Change and stability in the lives of young men.* Ann Arbor: University of Michigan, Institute for Social Research.

Bagley, C. (1989). Aggression and anxiety in day care graduates. *Psychological Reports*, *64*(250), 7.

Bartolke, K., Bergman, T., & Liegle, L. (Eds.). (1980). *Integrated cooperatives in the industrial society—the example of the kibbutz.* Assen, The Netherlands: Van Gorcum.

Barton, M., & Schwarz, J. (1981, August). *Day care in the middle class: Effects in elementary school.* Paper presented at the Convention of the American Psychological Association, Los Angeles.

Bar-Yam, M., Kohlberg, L., & Naame, A. (1980). Moral reasoning of students in different cultural, social and educational settings. *American Journal of Education, 88*(3), 345–362.

Baumrind, D. (1971). Current patterns of parental authority. *Developmental Psychology, 4*, 1–103.

Bearison, D. J., Magzamen, S., & Filardo, E. K. (1986). Socio–cognitive conflict and cognitive growth in young children. *Merrill Palmer Quarterly, 32*, 51–72.

Becker, H. S. (1973). *Outsiders: Studies in the sociology of deviance.* New York: Free Press.

Beitchman, J. H., Zucker, K. J., Hood, J. E., DaCosta, G. A., Akman, D., & Cassavia, E. (1992). A review of the long-term effects of child sexual abuse. *Child Abuse and Neglect, 16*(1), 101–118.

Bell, D. (1973). *The coming of post-industrial society: A venture in forecasting.* New York: Basic Books.

Belsky, J. (1988). The "effects" of infant day care reconsidered. *Early Childhood Research Quarterly, 3*, 235–272.

Belsky, J., & Steinberg, L. D. (1978). The effects of day care: A critical review. *Child Development, 49*, 929–949.

Ben-David, J. (1964). *Agricultural planning and village community in Israel.* Paris: United Nations Educational, Scientific, and Cultural Organization.

Ben-Yosef, A. (1963). *The purest democracy in the world.* London: Herzel Press.

Bergman, T. (1980). The replicability of the kibbutz experience. In K. Bartolke, T. Bergman, & L. Liegle (Eds.), *Integrated cooperatives in the industrial society—the example of the kibbutz* (pp. 227–236). Assen, The Netherlands: Van Gorcum.

Bersherov, D. J. (1977–1978). The legal aspects of reporting known and suspected child abuse and neglect. *Villanova Law Review, 23*(3), 458–520.

Bettelheim, B. (1969). *The children of the dream.* London: Macmillan.

Bianchi, S. M. (1984). Children's progress through school: A research note. *Sociology of Education, 57*, 184–192.

Blasi, J. (1977). The Israeli kibbutz: Economic efficiency and justice. *Community Development Journal, 12*(3), 201–210.

_____. (1978). *The communal future: The kibbutz and the utopian dilemma.* Norwood, PA: Norwood Editions.

Bowlby, J. (1965). *Child care and the growth of love.* Baltimore: Penguin.

Breitmayer, B. J., & Ramey, C. T. (1986). Biological nonoptimality and quality of postnatal environment as codeterminants of intellectual development. *Child Development, 57*, 1151–1165.

Broman, S. H., Nichols, P. L., & Kennedy, W. A. (1975). *Preschool IQ: Prenatal and early developmental correlates.* Hillsdale, NJ: Erlbaum.

Bronfenbrenner, U. (1970). *Two worlds of childhood: US and USSR.* New York: Russel Sage Foundation.

Buber, M. (1949). *Paths in utopia* (R. I. C. Hull, Trans.). Boston: Beacon.

Burchinal, M. R., Bryant, D. M., Lee, M. W., & Ramey, C. T. (1992). Early day care, infant-mother attachment, and maternal responsiveness in the infant's first year. *Early Childhood Research Quarterly, 7*(3), 383–396.

Charvet, J. (1969). The idea of equality as a substantive principle of society. *Political Studies, 27*(1), 1–13.

Cherns, A. (1980). The quality of working life and the community. In A. Cherns (Ed.), *Quality of working life and the kibbutz experience* (pp. 208–216). Norwood, PA: Norwood Editions.

Child pornography and pedophilia. (1986). A report made by Permanent Subcommittee on Investigations of the Committee on Governmental Affairs. Congress of the United States Senate Committee on Governmental Affairs. (ERIC Document Reproduction Service No. ED 275958)

Christiansen, K. O. (Ed.) (1965). *Scandinavian studies in criminology* (Vol. 1). London: Tavistock.

Clemmer, D. (1958). *The prison community.* New York: Rinehart.

Cloward, R. A., & Ohlin, L. E. (1960). *Delinquency and opportunity: A theory of delinquent gangs.* New York: Free Press.

Cohen, F. (1980). *The law of deprivation of liberty: A study in social control.* St. Paul, MN: West.

_____. (1982). *The law of deprivation of liberty supplement.* Albany, NY: State University of New York at Albany Graduate School of Criminal Justice.

Coopland, A. (1990). Infant mortality: Is prenatal care the answer? *Journal of Health Care for the Poor and Undeserved, 1*(3), 267–270.

Curtis, M., & Chertoff, M. S. (Eds.). (1973). *Israel, social structure, and social change.* New Brunswick, NJ: Transaction.

Cutthroat pre-meds. (1974, May 20). *Time.* p. 62.

Daniels, N. (1975). Equal liberty and unequal worth of liberty. In N. Daniels (Ed.), *Reading Rawls: Critical studies on Rawls' A theory of justice* (pp. 253–281). New York: Basic Books.

Davis, W., & McCaul, E. J. (1991). The emerging crises: Current and projected status of children in the United States. Orono, ME: Institute for the Study of At-Risk Students. (ERIC Document Reproduction Service No. ED 348434)

Davis, J. H., & Restle, F. (1963). The analysis of problems and prediction of group problem solving. *Journal of Abnormal Social Psychology, 66*(2), 103–116.

Dealing with dropouts: The urban superintendent's call to action (1987). Washington, DC: Office of Educational Research and Improvement, U. S. Department of Education.

Decourcey, P., & Decourcey, J. (1973). *A silent tragedy: Child abuse in the community.* Sherman Oaks, CA: Alfred.

Dentler, R. A., & Monroe, L. J. (1961). Social correlates of early adolescent theft. *American Sociological Review, 26,* 733–743.

Devereux, E. C., Shouval, R., Bronfenbrenner, U., Rodgers, R. R., Kav-Venaki, S., Kiely, E., & Karson, E. (1974). Socialization practices of parents, teachers, and peers in Israel: The kibbutz versus the city. *Child Development, 45,* 269–281.

Dinkins, D. (1990, January 2). Text of Dinkins' speech: We are all foot soldiers on the march to freedom. *The New York Times,* p. B-2.

Doherty, S. (1989, November 13). Teaching kids how to grieve: In L. A. it's never too early to learn. *Newsweek,* p. 73.

Dorrell, L. D. (1992). *Just take your time and keep it between the lines: Rural education and the at-risk student.* Paper presented at the Annual Convention of the National Rural Education Association, Traverse City, MI. (ERIC Document Reproduction Service No. ED 355073)

Drug abuse education and prevention programs for youth (1991). Congress of the United States, House Committee on Education and Labor. (ERIC Document Reproduction Service No. ED 338961)

Duffee, D. (1980). *Explaining criminal justice: Community theory and criminal justice reform.* Cambridge, MA: Oelgeschlager, Gunn & Hain.

Duffee, D., Hussey, F., & Kramer, J. (1978). *Criminal justice: Organization, structure and analysis.* Englewood Cliffs, NJ: Prentice Hall.

Durkheim, E. (1951). *Suicide: A study in sociology* (J. Spalding & G. Simpson, Trans.). New York: Free Press.

_____. (1961). *Moral education: A study in the theory and application in the sociology of education* (E. K. Wilson & H. Schnurer, Trans.). New York: Free Press.

Dworkin, R. (1975). The original position. In N. Daniels (Ed.), *Reading Rawls: Critical studies on Rawls' A theory of justice* (pp. 16–52). New York: Basic Books.

Eckenrode, J., Laird, M., & Doris, J. (1993). School performance and disciplinary problems among abused and neglected children. *Developmental Psychology, 29*(1), 53–62.

Eden, D. B. (1975). Intrinsic and extrinsic rewards and motives: Replication and extension with kibbutz workers. *Journal of Applied Social Psychology, 5*(4), 348–361.

_____. (1980). Assessment. In A. Cherns (Ed.), *Quality of working life and the kibbutz experience* (pp. 270–275). Norwood, PA: Norwood Editions.

Eden, D. B., & Leviatan, U. (1974). Farm and factory in the kibbutz: A study in agrico-industrial psychology. *Journal of Applied Psychology, 59*(5), 596–602.

Eiferman, R. (1970). Cooperativeness and egalitarianism in kibbutz children's games. *Human Relations, 26*(6), 579–587.

Eisenberg, L. (1965). Mental health issues in Israeli collectives: Kibbutzim. *Journal of the American Academy of Child Psychiatry, 4*(3), 426–442.

_____. (1991). What's happening to American families? Urbana, Il: ERIC Clearinghouse on Elementary and Early Childhood Education. (ERIC Document Reproduction Service No. ED 330496)

Eisenberg, L., & Kanner, L. (1956). Early infantile autism 1943–55. *American Journal of Orthopsychiatry, 26,* 556–566.

Ellenwood, A. E., Majsterek, D., & Jones. E. D. (1991). Runaways: A silent crisis. Paper presented at the National Conference on Troubled Adolescents, Milwaukee, WI. (ERIC Document Reproduction No. ED 332114)

Elliott, D. S., & Voss, H. L. (1974). *Delinquency and dropout.* Lexington MA: Lexington Books.

Elmhorn, K. (1965). Study in self-reported delinquency among school children in Stockholm. In K. O. Christiansen (Ed.), *Scandinavian studies in criminology* (Vol. 1) (pp. 117–146). London: Tavistock.

Emery, K. J. (1993). Position statement on youth violence: Prevention and recommended actions. Dayton, OH: New Futures for Dayton Area Youth Inc. (ERIC Document Reproduction Service No. ED 357091)

Engels, F. (1942). *The origins of the family, private property, and the state.* New York: International Publishers.

Erickson, M. F., Sroufe, L. A., & Egeland, B. (1985). The relationship between quality of attachment and behavior problems in preschool in a high-risk sample. In I. Bretherton & E. Waters (Eds.), *Growing points in attachment theory and research* (pp. 147–166). *Monographs of the Society for Research in Child Development, 50* (Serial No. 209).

Farran, D. (1982). Now for the bad news. *Annual Editions: Early Childhood Education, 83/84,* 88–90.

Farran, D. C., Haskins, R., & Gallagher, J. J. (1980). Poverty and mental retardation: A search for explanations. In J. J. Gallagher (Ed.), *Ecology of exceptional children.* San Francisco: Jossey-Bass.

Farrington, D. P. (1973). Self-reports of deviant behavior: Predictive and stable. *Journal of Criminal Law and Criminology, 64,* 99–110.

Fein, G. G., & Fox, N. (1988). Infant day care: A special issue. *Early Childhood Research Quarterly, 3,* 227–234.

Finkelhor, D. (1993). Epidemiological factors in the clinical identification of child sexual abuse. *Child Abuse and Neglect, 17,* 67–70.

Fisk, M. (1975). History and reason in Rawls' "moral theory". In N. Daniels (Ed.), *Reading Rawls: Critical studies on Rawls' A theory of justice* (pp. 53–80). New York: Basic Books.

Flacks, R. (1978). Growing up confused: Cultural crises and individual character. In Krisberg, B. & Austin J. (Eds.), *The children of Ishmael: Critical perspectives on juvenile justice: A text with readings* (pp. 231–242). Palo Alto: Mayfield.

Flowers, R. B. (1986). The adolescent victim of crime and delinquency. Washington, DC: U. S. Dept. of Education, Office of Educational Research. (ERIC Document Reproduction Service No. ED 285059)

Footlick, J. K. (1990, Winter/Spring). What happened to the family? *Newsweek,* Vol. *CXIV*(27), pp. 14–20.

Forty-eight hours (1991, March 20: 8–9 P.M. CBS television program.

Foss, B. M. (Ed.) (1969). *Determinants of infant behavior* (Vol. 4). London: Methuen.

Galinsky, E. (1990a). The costs of not providing quality early childhood programs. *Annual Editions: Early Childhood Education, 91/92,* 233–240.

_____. (1990b). From our president. I have seen the beginnings of a transformation in attitudes. *Young Children, 45*(6), 2.

_____. (1990c). *Reaching the full cost of quality in early childhood programs.* Washington, DC: National Association for the Education of Young Children.

Galston, W. A. (1993). Causes of declining well-being among U. S. children. *Aspen Institute Quarterly, 5*(1), 52–77.

Gamson, Z. F., & Palgi, M. (1982). The "over-educated" kibbutz: Shifting relations between social reproduction and individual development on the kibbutz. *Interchange, 13*(1), 55–67.

Garland, B. K. (1985). The possible effects of nutritional status and growth of children on the economic potential of West Virginia. (ERIC Document Reproduction Service No. ED 275483)

Gelles, R., & Strauss, M. (1979). Violence in the American family. *Journal of Social Issues, 35,* 15–39.

Gewirth, A. (1978). *Reason and morality.* Chicago: University of Chicago Press.

Gilligan, C. (1980). The effects of social institutions on the moral development of children and adolescents. *Bulletin of the Menninger Clinic, 44*(5), 498–523.

Glaser, D. (1964). *Effectiveness of a prison and parole system.* Indianapolis: Bobbs-Merrill.

Glueck, S., & Glueck, E. (1950). *Unraveling juvenile delinquency.* Cambridge, MA: Harvard University Press.

_____. (1972). *Identification of pre-delinquents: Validation studies and some suggested uses of Glueck table.* New York: Intercontinental Medical Book Corp.

Goffman, E. (1961). *Asylums: Essays on the social situation of mental patients and other inmates.* Chicago: Aldine.

Goins, B., & Cesarone, B. (1993). Homeless children: Meeting the educational challenges. Urbana, IL: ERIC Clearinghouse on Elementary and Early Childhood Education. (ERIC Document Reproduction Service No. ED 356099)

Golden, M., & Birns, B. (1983). Social class and infant intelligence. In M. Lewis (Ed.), *Origins of intelligence* (2nd ed.) (pp. 347–398). New York: Plenum.

Golden, M., Rosenbluth, L., Grossi, M., Policare, H., Freeman, H., & Brownlee, E. (1978). *The New York City infant day care study.* New York: Medical and Health Research Association of New York City.

Golomb, N. (1980). The relations between the kibbutz and its industry. In A. Cherns (Ed.), *Quality of working life and the kibbutz experience: Proceedings of an international conference in Israel, June 1978* (pp. 84–90). Norwood, PA: Norwood Editions.

Goodman, P. (1960). *Growing up absurd: Problems of youth in the organized system.* New York: Random House.

Gove, W. R. (Ed.) (1980). *The labelling of deviance.* Beverly Hills: Sage.

Green, A. W. (1946). The middle class male child and neurosis. *American Sociological Review, 11*(1), 31–41.

Hafen, B. (1976). Children's liberation and the new egalitarianism: Some reservations about abandoning youth to their "rights." *Brigham Young University Law Review, 1976,* 605–658.

Hare R. M. (1975). Rawls' theory of justice. In N. Daniels (Ed.), *Reading Rawls: Critical studies on Rawls' A theory of justice* (pp. 81–107). New York: Basic Books.

Harlow, H. F., & Harlow, M. K. (1969). Effects of various mother-infant relationships on rhesus monkey behaviors. In B. M. Foss (Ed.), *Determinants of infant behavior* (Vol. 4) (pp. 15–36). London: Methuen.

Hart, H. L. (1975). Rawls on liberty and its priority. In N. Daniels (Ed.), *Reading Rawls: Critical studies on Rawls' A theory of justice* (pp. 230–252). New York: Basic Books.

Hartup, W. (1970). Peer interaction and social organization. In P.H. Mussen (Ed.), *Carmichael's manual of child psychology* (pp. 361–456). New York: John Wiley & Sons.

Hawkins, S. (1985, March 11). Rat pack youth: Teenage rebels in suburbia. *U. S. News and World Report*, pp. 51–54.

Healthy children: Investing in the future (1988). Congress of the United States, Office of Technology Assessment. Washington, DC: U.S. Government Printing Office.

Hechinger, F. M. (1989, November 22). A new study suggests that early childhood education should proceed gently. *The New York Times*, p. B–11.

Heflin, L. J., & Rudy, K. (1991). Homeless and in need of special education: Exceptional children at risk. Reston, VA: Council for Exceptional Children. (ERIC Document Reproduction Service No. ED 339167)

Helfer, R. E., & Kempe, C. H. (Eds.) (1976). *Child abuse and neglect: The family and the community.* Cambridge, MA: Ballinger.

Hesov, L. A., & Berger, M. (Eds.) (1978). *Aggression and antisocial behavior in childhood and adolescence.* New York: Pergamon.

Hetherton, E. M., Cox, M., & Cox, R. (1982). Effects of divorce on parents and children. In M. Lamb (Ed.), *Nontraditional families: Parenting and child development* (pp. 233-288). Hillsdale, NJ: Erlbaum.

Hindelang, M. J. (1978). Race and involvement in common law personal crimes. *American Sociological Review, 43,* 93–109.

Hindelang, M. J., Hirschi T., & Weis, J. (1979) Correlates of delinquency: The illusion of discrepancy between self-report and official measures. *American Sociological Review, 44,* 995–1014.

_____. (1981). *Measuring delinquency.* Beverly Hills: Sage.

Hindelang, M. J., & Weis, J. (1972). The bc-try cluster and factor analysis system: Personality and self-reported delinquency. *Criminology, 10,* 268–294.

Hirschi, T. (1969). *Causes of delinquency.* Berkeley, CA: University of California Press.

_____. (1978). Causes and prevention of delinquency. In H. M. Johnson (Ed.), *Social system and legal process: Theory, comparative perspectives, and special studies.* San Francisco: Jossey-Bass.

_____. (1980). Labelling theory and juvenile delinquency: An assessment of the evidence. In W. R. Gove (Ed.), *The labelling of deviance* (pp. 271–302). Beverly Hills: Sage.

Hirschi T., & Selvin, H. C. (1967). *Delinquency research: An appraisal of analytic methods.* New York: Free Press.

Hobbs, F., & Lippman, L. (1990). *Children's well-being: An international comparison.* Washington, DC: Select Committee on Children, Youth, and Families. (ERIC Document Reproduction Service No. ED 321842)

Hofferth, S. L. (1989, August). Mothers versus children: The real child care debate. Swarthmore College Bulletin, pp. 10–11.

Horn, R. (1984, April 12). Youth Aliyah at 50. *The Jewish World,* pp. 11, 14.

Hoyle, J. R. (1993). Our children: Dropouts, pushouts, and burnouts. *People and Education, 1*(1), 26–41.

Hume, D. (1978). *A treatise of human nature.* Oxford: Clarendon Press. (Original work published 1739)

Huston, A. C. (1989). *Consequences of family change for children's development.* Paper presented at the Biennial Meeting of the Society for Research in Childhood Development, Kansas City, MO.

Irwin, J. (1970). *The felon.* Englewood Cliffs, NJ: Prentice Hall.

Jarus, A., Marcus, J., Oren J., & Rapaport C. (Eds.). (1970). *Children and families in Israel: Some mental health perspectives.* New York: Gordon & Breach.

Jason, J. (1984). Centers for disease control and the epidemiology of violence. *Child Abuse and Neglect, 8,* 279–283.

Jay, J., & Birney, R. C. (1973). Research findings on the kibbutz adolescents: A response to Bettelheim. *American Journal of Orthopsychiatry, 43*(3), 347–354.

Johnson, H. M. (Ed.) (1978). *Social system and legal process: Theory, comparative perspectives, and special studies.* San Francisco: Jossey-Bass.

Judicial training and research for child custody litigation. (1992). Washington, DC: Congress of the United States, House Committee on the Judiciary. (ERIC Document Reproduction Service No. ED 352177)

Kagan, S. (1990). *Excellence in early childhood education: Defining characteristics and next-decade strategies.* Washington, DC: Outreach Staff of Information Services, Office of Educational Research and Improvement.

Kagan, S., & Zigler, E. (Eds.). (1987). *Early schooling: The national debate.* New Haven: Yale University Press.

Kahane, R. (1975). The committed: Preliminary reflections on the impact of the kibbutz socialization pattern on adolescents. *British Journal of Sociology, 26,* 343–353.

Kamisar, Y. (1981). *Modern criminal procedure.* St. Paul, MN: West.

Kantor, D. (1988, April 14). Changes noted in kibbutzim. *The Jewish World,* p. 16.

Katz, D. (1980). Epilogue. In U. Leviatan & M. Rosner (Eds.), *Work and organization in kibbutz industry* (pp. 193–204). Norwood, PA: Norwood Editions.

Katz, S. N. (1971). *When parents fail: The law's response to family breakdown.* Boston: Beacon.

Kibbutz Conference. (1992, November). Center for Kibbutz Studies. Boston: Harvard University.

Kids count: Data book: State profiles of child well-being (1993). Washington, DC: Center for the Study of Social Policy. (ERIC Document Reproduction Service No. ED 357110)

Kohlberg, L. (1971). Cognitive development theory and the practice of collective moral education. In M. Wolins & M. Gottesmann (Eds.), *Group care: An Israeli approach* (pp. 342–371). New York: Gordon & Breach.

_____. (1975, June). The cognitive-developmental approach to moral education. *Phi Delta Kappan*, 670–677.

_____. (1979). Justice as reversibility. In P. Laslett & J. Fishkin (Eds.), *Philosophy, politics and society* (pp. 257–272). New Haven: Yale University Press.

Kolata, G. (1989, August 11). In cities poor families are dying of crack. *The New York Times*, pp. A-1, A-13.

Kornhauser, R. R. (1978). *Social sources of delinquency: An appraisal of analytic models*. Chicago: University of Chicago Press.

Kozol, J. (1990, Winter/Spring). The new untouchables. *Newsweek*, Vol. *CXIV*(27), pp. 48–53.

Krisberg, B., & Austin, J. (Eds.). (1978). *The children of Ishmael: Critical perspectives on juvenile justice: A text with readings*. Palo Alto: Mayfield.

Kulik, J. A., Stein, K. B., & Sarbin, T. R. (1968a). Dimensions and patterns of adolescent antisocial behavior. *Journal of Consulting and Clinical Psychology, 32*, 375–382.

_____. (1968b). Disclosure of delinquent behavior under conditions of anonymity and non-anonymity. *Journal of Consulting and Clinical Psychology, 32*, 506–509.

Lemert, E. (1972). *Human deviance, social problems, and social control* (2nd ed.). Englewood Cliffs, NJ: Prentice Hall.

Leon, D. (1969). *The kibbutz: A new way of life.* Oxford: Pergamon Press.

Leviatan, U. (1973). The industrial process in the Israeli kibbutzim: Problems and their solutions. In M. Curtis & M. S. Chertoff (Eds.), *Israel: Social structure and change* (pp. 159–171). New Brunswick, NJ: Transaction.

_____. (1976). The process of industrialization in the Israeli kibbutzim. In J. Nash, H. J. Dandler, & N. S. Hopkins (Eds.), *Popular participation in the social change cooperatives, collectives and nationalized industry* (pp. 521–547). The Hague: Mouton Pub.

_____. (1982). Higher education in the Israeli kibbutz: Revolution and effect. *Interchange, 13*(1), 68–82.

Leviatan, U., & Rosner, M. (1980). Summary: Lessons from research on kibbutz industrialization. In U. Leviatan & M. Rosner (Eds.), *Work and organization in kibbutz industry* (pp. 184–211). Norwood, PA: Norwood Editions.

Levitan, S. A., & Schillmoeller, S. (1991). The paradox of homelessness in America. Washington, DC: George Washington University, Center for Social Policy Studies. (ERIC Document Reproduction Service No. ED 328759)

Lewin, K. (1942). Field theory of learning: Selected theoretical papers. In N. B. Henry (Ed.), *Yearbook: National Society for the Study of Education, Committee on The Psychology of Learning,* 41st, part 2 (pp. 215–242). Chicago: University of Chicago Press.

_____. (1951). *Field theory in social science: Selected theoretical papers.* New York: Harper.

Lewis, M. (Ed.) (1976). *Origins of intelligence.* New York: Plenum.

Locke, J. (1960). *Two treatises of government.* Cambridge, England: Cambridge University Press. (Original work published 1698)

Macarov. D. (1972). Work patterns and satisfactions in an Israeli kibbutz: A test of the Hertzberg hypothesis. *Personnel Psychology,* 25, 483–493.

Margolin, L. (1992). Child abuse by mothers' boyfriends: Why the overrepresentation? *Child Abuse and Neglect,* 16(4), 541–545.

Marshner, C. (1988, May 13). Is day care good for kids? *National Review,* p. 30.

McCallum, J. (1980). Co-operative solidarity: A theoretical perspective. In A. Cherns (Ed.), *Quality of working life and the kibbutz experience* (pp. 107–117). Norwood, PA: Norwood Editions.

McCord, W., McCord, J. & Zola, I. K. (1959). *Origins of crime.* New York: Columbia University Press.

McCormick, K. (1989). An equal chance: Educating at-risk children to succeed. Alexandria, VA: National School Boards Association. (ERIC Document Reproduction No. ED 307359)

Mead, M. (1954). Some theoretical considerations on the problem of mother-infant separation. *American Journal of Orthopsychiatry,* 24, 471–483.

Messinger, S. L. (1969). Issues in the study of the social system of prison inmates. *Issues in Criminology,* 4(2), 133–144.

Michaelman, F. (1975). Constitutional welfare rights and a theory of justice. In N. Daniels (Ed.), *Reading Rawls: Critical studies on Rawls' A theory of justice* (pp. 319–346). New York: Basic Books.

Miller, R. W. (1975). Rawls and Marxism. In N. Daniels (Ed.), *Reading Rawls: Critical studies on Rawls' A theory of justice* (pp. 206–230). New York: Basic Books.

Miller, L. B., & Bizzell, R. P. (1984). Long-term effects of four preschool programs: Ninth- and tenth-grade results. *Child Development,* 55, 1570–1587.

Miller, M., & Miller, J. (1978). The plague of domestic violence in the U.S. *U.S.A. Today,* 108, p. 26.

Mills, J. S. (1926). *On liberty and other essays.* New York: MacMillan.

Milne, A. M., Myers, D. E., Rosenthal, A. S., & Ginsberg, A. (1986). Single parents, working mothers, and the educational achievement of children. *Sociology of Education,* 59, 125–139.

Mittler, P. (Ed.) (1977). *Research to practice in mental retardation, Vol. 1: Care and intervention.* Baltimore: University Park Press.

Moore, R., Pauker, J. D., & Moore, T. E. (1984). Delinquent recidivists: Vulnerable children. *Journal of Youth and Adolescence,* 13, 451–457.

Moses, C. E., & Kopplin, D. (1992). Applying humanistic principles to the treatment of runaway and throwaway adolescents. Paper presented at the Annual Convention of the Southwestern Psychological Association, Austin Texas. (ERIC Document Reproduction No. ED 345171)

Moynihan, D. P. (1988, September 25). Half the nation's children born without a fair chance. *The New York Times*, p. E-25.

Murphy, D. F. (1988). The just community at Birch Meadow elementary school. *Phi Delta Kappan*, *69*(6), 427–428.

Naagi, S. Z. (1977). *Child maltreatment in the United States: A challenge to social institutions.* New York: Columbia University Press.

Nadler, A. Romek, E., & Shapira-Friedman, A. (1979). Giving in the kibbutz: Prosocial behavior of city and kibbutz children affected by social responsibility and social pressure. *Journal of Cross Cultural Psychology*, *10*(1), 57–72.

Nash, J., Dandler, H. J., & Hopkins, N. S. (Eds.) (1976). *Popular participation in the social change cooperatives, collectives and nationalized industry.* The Hague: Mouton.

National Advisory Commission on Criminal Justice Standards and Goals (1976). *Juvenile justice and delinquency prevention: A report of the task force on juvenile justice and delinquency prevention.* Washington, DC: U. S. Government Printing Office.

National Association for the Education of Young Children (1985). In whose hands? A demographic fact sheet on child care providers. Washington, DC: Author.

Natriello, G., McDill, E. L., & Pallas, A. M. (1990). Schooling disadvantaged children: Racing against catastrophe. New York: Teachers College Press, Columbia University.

Near, H. (1982). Kibbutz education: An historical approach. *Interchange*, *13*(1), 3–15.

Neiman, R. H., & Gastright, J. F. (1981). The long-term effects of Title I preschool and all-day kindergarten. *Phi Delta Kappan*, *63*, 184–186.

Neubauer, P. B. (Ed.) (1965). *Children in collectives, child-rearing aims and practices in the kibbutz.* Springfield Il: Thomas.

Nielsen, K. (1985). *Equality and liberty: A defense of radical egalitarianism.* Totowa, NJ: Rowman & Allanheld.

Nill, C. (1978). Youth as a crime-generating phenomena. In B. Krisberg & J. Austin (Eds.), *The children of Ishmael: Critical perspectives on juvenile justice: A text with readings* (pp. 221–230). Palo Alto: Mayfield.

Nozick, R. (1974). *Anarchy, state and utopia.* New York: Basic Books.

Nye, F. I. (1958). *Family relationships and delinquent behavior.* New York: Wiley.

Nye, F. I., & Short, J. F. (1957). Scaling delinquent behavior. *American Sociological Review*, *22*, 326–331.

Office of Juvenile Justice and Delinquency Prevention (1991) Annual report. Washington, DC: U. S. Department of Justice, Office of Justice Programs, Office of Juvenile Justice and Delinquency Prevention.

Olsen, D., & Zigler, E. (1988). An assessment of the all-day kindergarten movement. *Early Childhood Research Quarterly*, *4*, 167–186.

O'Neill, O., & Ruddick, W. (1979). *Having children: Philosophical and legal reflections on parenthood.* New York: Oxford University Press.

Peffer, R. (1978). A defense of rights to well-being. *Philosophy and Public Affairs, 8*(1), 65–87.

Phillips, S. (1986). Children in blended and step families. Kinsington, Australia: Foundation for Child and Youth Studies. (ERIC Document Reproduction Service No. ED 286579)

Piaget, J. (1966). *The moral judgement of the child* (M. Gabois, Trans.). New York: Free Press.

Plato. (1965). *The republic of Plato* (F. M. Cornford, Trans.). New York: Oxford University Press. (Original work undated)

_____. (1979). *Plato: Gorgias* (T. Irwin, Trans). Oxford, England: Clarendon. (Original work undated)

Powers, J. L., Eckenrode, J., & Jaklitsch, B. (1990). Maltreatment among runaway and homeless youth. *Child Abuse and Neglect, 14*(1), 87–98.

President's Commission on Law Enforcement and the Administration of Justice (1967). *Task force report: Juvenile delinquency and youth crime.* Washington, DC: U.S. Government Printing Office.

Rabin, A. I. (1957). Personality maturity of kibbutz (Israeli collective settlement) and non-kibbutz children as reflected in Rorschach findings. *Journal of Projective Techniques, 21,* 148–153.

_____. (1958a). Infants and children under conditions of "intermittent" mothering in the kibbutz. *American Journal of Orthopsychiatry, 28*(3), 557–584.

_____. (1958b). Some psychosexual differences between kibbutz and non-kibbutz Israeli boys. *Journal of Projective Techniques, 22,* 328–332.

_____. (1959). Attitudes of kibbutz children in family and parents. *American Journal of Orthopsychiatry, 29,* 172–179.

_____. (1965). *Growing up in the kibbutz: Comparison of the personality of children brought up in the kibbutz and of family-reared children.* New York: Springer.

Rafferty, Y., & Shinn, M. (1991). The impact of homelessness on children. *American Psychologist, 46*(11), 1170–1179.

Ramey, C. T., & Campbell, F. (1977). The prevention of developmental retardation in high-risk children. In P. Mittler (Ed.), *Research to practice in mental retardation, Vol. 1: Care and intervention.* Baltimore: University Park Press.

Ramey, C. T., & Finkelstein, N. W. (1978). Contingent stimulation and infant competence. *Journal of Pediatric Psychology, 3,* 89–96.

Ramey, C. T., Dorval, B., & Baker-Ward, L. (1983). Group day care and socially disadvantaged families: Effects on the child and the family. In S. Kilmer (Ed.), *Advances in Early Education and Day Care* (Vol. 3) (pp. 69-106). New York: JAI Press.

Rawls, J. (1971). *A theory of justice.* Cambridge, MA: Harvard University Press.

_____. (1977). The basic structure as subject. *American Philosophical Quarterly, 14*(2), 159–176.

_____. (1980). Kantian constructivism in moral philosophy: Rational and full autonomy. *Journal of Philosophy, 77*(9), 515–577.

Redl, F. (1965). Pathogenic factors in the modern child's life. In P. B. Neubauer (Ed.), *Children in collectives*, (pp. 269–279). Springfield, Il: Thomas.

Riesman, D. (1950). *The lonely crowd*. New Haven: Yale University Press.

Reimer, J. (1972) . The development of moral character in the kibbutzim with a special focus on adolescents, mimeographed. Cambridge, MA: Harvard University.

Reyone, N. D. (1993). A comparison of the school performance of sexually abused, neglected, and non-maltreated children. *Child Study Journal*, *23*(1), 17–38.

Rodman, H., & Grams, P. (1967). Juvenile delinquency and the family: A review and discussion. In *President's Commission on Law Enforcement and the Administration of Justice*, Task force report: Juvenile delinquency and youth crime. Washington, DC: U.S. Government Printing Office.

Rosner, M. (1970). Commutarian experiment, self-management experience and the kibbutz. *Group Process*, *3*(1), 79–100.

_____. (1973). Worker participation in decision making in kibbutz industry. In M. Curtis & M. Chertoff (Eds.), *Israel, social structure, and social change* (pp. 145–157). New Brunswick. NJ: Transaction.

_____. (1980). The quality of working life in the kibbutz. In A. Cherns (Ed.), *Quality of working life and the kibbutz experience* (pp. 132–144). Norwood, PA: Norwood Editions.

Rousseau, J. J. (1947). *The social contract*. New York: Hafen. (Original work published 1762)

Rubin, K. H., Fein, G. G., & Vandenberg, B. (1983). Play. In E. M. Hetherington (Ed.), *Handbook of child psychology: Socialization, personality, and social development* (Vol. 4). New York: Wiley.

Sabotta, E. E., & Davis, R. L. (1992). Fatality after report to a child abuse registry in Washington State, 1973–1986. *Child Abuse and Neglect 16*(5), 627–635.

Sandel, M. J. (1982). *Liberalism and the limits of justice*. New York: Cambridge University Press.

Sariola, H., & Uutela, A. (1992). The prevalence and context of family violence against children in Finland. *Child Abuse and Neglect*, *16*(6), 823–832.

Scanlon, T. M. (1975). Rawls' theory of justice. In N. Daniels (Ed.), *Reading Rawls: Critical studies on Rawls' A theory of justice* (pp. 169–207). New York: Basic Books.

Schloesser, P. (1992). Active surveillance of child abuse fatalities. *Child Abuse and Neglect*, *16*(1), 3–10. (ERIC Document Reproduction No. ED 444408)

Schneewind, J. B. (1967). Henry Sidgwick. In P. Edwards (Ed.), *Encyclopedia of philosophy* (Vol. 7) 434–436. New York & London: MacMillan, Free Press, & Collier-MacMillan.

Schorr, L. B. (1988). *Within our reach: Breaking the Cycle of Disadvantage*. New York: Doubleday.

Schur, E. M. (1973). *Radical non-intervention: Rethinking the delinquency problem*. Englewood Cliffs, NJ: Prentice Hall.

Schwartz, P. (1983). Length of day-care attendance and attachment behavior in eighteen-month-old infants. *Child Development*, *54*, 1073–1078.

Schwarz, J. C. (1983, April). *Effects of group day care in the first two years.* Paper presented at the biennial meetings of the Society for Research in Child Development: Detroit.

Schwarz, J. C., Krolick, G., & Strickland, R. G. (1973). Effects of early day care experience on adjustment to a new environment. *American Journal of Orthopsychiatry, 43,* 340–346.

Schwarz, J. C., Strickland, R. G., & Krolick, G. (1974). Infant day care: Behavioral effects at preschool age. *Developmental Psychology, 10,* 502–506.

Seligmann, J. (1990, Winter/Spring). Variations on a theme. *Newsweek,* Vol. *CXIV*(27), pp. 38–46.

Sellin, T., & Wolfgang, M. (1964). *The measurement of delinquency.* New York: Wiley.

Selltiz, C., & Society for the Psychological Study of Social Issues. (1959). *Research methods in social relations.* New York: Holt, Rinehart, & Winston.

Seltzner, J. A. (1992). *Crises at a Bronx junior high: Responding to school-related violence.* Paper presented at the Annual Convention of the American Psychological Association, Washington, DC.

Shapira, A., & Madsen, M. C. (1969). Cooperative and competitive behavior of kibbutz and urban children in Israel. *Child Development, 40,* 609–618.

Shaw, M. (1932). A comparison of individuals and small groups in the rational solution of complex problems, *American Journal of Psychology, 44*(1), 491–504.

Shaw, M. E. (1981). *Group dynamics: The psychology of small group behavior* (3rd ed.). New York: McGraw-Hill.

Short, J. F., & Nye. F. I. (1958). Extent of unrecorded juvenile delinquency: Tentative conclusions. *Journal of Criminal Law and Criminology, 409,* 296–302.

Sidgwick, H. (1907). *The methods of ethics* (7th ed.). London: MacMillan.

Siegel, L. J., & Senna, J. J. (1994). *Juvenile delinquency: Theory, practice and law.* St. Paul, MN: West Pub. Co.

Sigel, I. (1987). Early childhood education: Developmental enhancement or developmental acceleration. In S. Kagan & E. Zigler (Eds.), *Early schooling: The national debate* (pp. 129-151). New Haven: Yale University Press.

Sourcebook of criminal justice statistics 1975 (1976). U.S. Dept. of Justice, Bureau of Justice Statistics. Washington, DC: U.S. Government Printing Office.

Sourcebook of criminal justice statistics 1987 (1988). U.S. Dept. of Justice, Bureau of Justice Statistics. Washington, DC: U.S. Government Printing Office.

Sourcebook of criminal justice statistics 1989 (1990). U.S. Dept. of Justice, Bureau of Justice Statistics. Washington, DC: U.S. Government Printing Office.

Spiro, M. E. (1972). *Kibbutz: Venture in utopia.* New York: Schocken Books.

Spitz, R. (1946). Anaclitic depression. *The Psychoanalytic Study of the Child, 2,* 313–347.

Sroufe, L. A. (1988). A developmental perspective on day care. *Early Childhood Research Quarterly*, *3*, 283–291.

Sroufe, L. A., & Fleeson, J. (1986). Attachment and the construction of relationships. In W. W. Hartup & Z. Rubin (Eds.), *Relationships and development*. Hillside, NJ: Erlbaum.

Statistical abstract of Israel 1989. (1989). Jerusalem: Ministry of the Interior, Government Printing Office, Central Bureau of Statistics.

Statistical abstract of the United States 1922. (1923), No. 45. Washington, DC: Dept. of Commerce, Bureau of Foreign and Domestic Commerce.

Statistical abstract of the United States 1987. (1987), No. 107. Washington, DC: U. S. Dept. of Commerce, Bureau of the Census.

Statistical abstract of the United States 1989. (1989), No. 109. Washington, DC: U. S. Dept. of Commerce, Bureau of the Census.

Statistical abstract of the United States 1990. (1990), No. 110. Washington, DC: U. S. Dept. of Commerce, Bureau of the Census.

Statistical abstract of the United States 1991. (1991), No. 111. Washington, DC: U. S. Dept. of Commerce, Bureau of the Census.

Statistical abstract of the United States 1992. (1992), No. 112. Washington, DC: U. S. Dept. of Commerce, Bureau of the Census.

Statistical abstract of the United States 1993. (1993), No. 113. Washington, DC: U. S. Dept. of Commerce, Bureau of the Census.

Stedman, J. B., Salganik, L. H., & Celebuski, C. A. (1988). Dropping out: The educational vulnerability of at-risk youth. Washington, DC: Congress Research Service.

Stone, J. (1991). Caregiver responsive language and related caregiving practices. Doctoral dissertation. University of Miami, 1991). *Dissertation Abstracts International*, *52*, p. 12A.

_____. (1993). Caregiver and teacher language: Responsive or restrictive? *Young Children*, *48*(4), 12–18.

Sykes, G. (1958). *The society of captives: A study of a maximum security prison*. Atheneum: New York.

Sykes, G. M., & Matza, D. (1957). Techniques of neutralization: A theory of delinquency. *American Sociological Review*, *22*, 664–670.

Talmon-Garber, Y. (1972). *Family and community in the kibbutz*. Cambridge, MA: Harvard University Press.

Tannenbaum, A. S. (1980). Foreword. In U. Leviatan & M. Rosner (Eds.), *Work and organization in kibbutz industry* (pp. XIII–XIX). Norwood, PA: Norwood Editions.

Tannenbaum, A. S., Kaucic, B., Rosner, M., Vianello, M., & Wieser, G. (1974). *Hierarchy in organizations: An international comparison*. San Francisco: Jossey-Bass.

Tannenbaum, F. (1938). *Crime and the community*. Boston: Ginn & Co.

Terr, L. (1981). Forbidden games: Post-traumatic child's play. *Journal of American Academy of Child Psychiatry*, *20*, 741–760.

_____. (1983). Chowchilla revisited: The effects of psychic trauma four years after a schoolbus kidnapping. *American Journal of Psychiatry*, *140*, 1543–1550.

Terry, D. (1992, Oct. 17). Even school is no refuge from gunfire and death. *The New York Times,* p. A-6.

Thompson, R. A. (1988). The effects of infant day care through the prism of attachment theory: A critical appraisal. *Early Childhood Research Quarterly, 3,* 273–282.

Thornberry, T. (1973). Race, socio-economic status, and sentencing in the juvenile justice system. *The Journal of Criminal Law and Criminology, 64*(1), 90–98.

_____. (1979). Sentencing disparities in the juvenile justice system. *The Journal of Criminal Law and Criminology, 70*(2), 164–171.

Timm, J. T. (1981). Group care of children and the development of moral judgment. *Child Welfare, 59*(6), 323–333.

Toffler, A. (1971). *Future shock.* New York: Bantam.

Toufexis, A. (1989, June 12). Our violent kids: A rise in brutal crimes by the young shakes the soul of society. *Time,* pp. 52–58.

Turiel, E. (1980). A cross-cultural study of moral development in Turkey and the United States, Unpublished manuscript.

_____. (1986). Social reasoning and childhood aggression. In D. H. Crowell, I. M. Evans, & C. R. O'Donnell (Eds.), *Childhood aggression and violence: Sources of influence, prevention and control,* (pp. 104–109). New York: Plenum.

Turiel, E., Edwards, C. P., & Kohlberg, L. (1978). Moral development in Turkish children, adolescents, and young adults *Journal of Cross-Cultural Psychology, 9*(1), 75–86.

Ulrich, E. (1980). On the relations between work experience and personality development. In A. Cherns (Ed.), *Quality of working life and the kibbutz experience* (pp. 217–229). Norwood, PA: Norwood Editions.

The unfinished agenda: A new vision for child development and education. A statement by the Research and Policy Committee of the Committee for Economic Development (1991). New York: Committee for Economic Development. (ERIC Document Reproduction Service No. ED 336444)

United Nations, General Assembly Resolution 1386 (XIV), adopted Nov. 20, 1959 (1960). *Official records of the General Assembly, 14th session,* Supp. No. 16, p. 20. New York: United Nations.

Van Biema, D. (1993, December 27). Robbing the innocents: A spate of murder-kidnappings raises alarm among parents. What can be done? *Time,* pp. 31–32.

Wadsworth, J., Burnell, J., Taylor, B., & Butler, N. (1985). The influence of family type on children's behaviour and development at five years. *Journal of Child Psychology and Psychiatry and Allied Disciplines, 26*(2), 245–254.

Wallach, L. B. (1993). Helping children cope with violence. *Young Children, 48*(4), 4–11.

Wallerstein, J. S., & Kelley, J. B. (1980). *Surviving the breakup: How children and parents cope with divorce.* New York: Basic Books.

Warren, R. (1978). *Community in America* (3rd ed.). Chicago: Rand McNally.

Wasserman, E. R. (1976). Implementing Kohlberg's "just community concept" in an alternative high school. *Social Education, 40*(4), 203–207.

Webber, R. P. (1988). *Step Families*. Wellington, Australia: Australian Council for Educational Research. (ERIC Document Reproduction Service No. ED 301778)

Weikart, D. P. (1983). A longitudinal view of a preschool research effort. In M. Perlmutter (Ed.), *Minnesota symposia on child psychology* (Vol. 16). Hillsdale, NJ: Erlbaum.

Weisberg, P. G. (1988). *Symposium: Social implications and alternatives for families and children in the next decade*. Paper presented at the Association for Childhood Education International Convention, Salt Lake City, Utah.

Werner, E. E. (1986). A longitudinal study of perinatal risk. In D. C. Farran & J. D. McKinney (Eds.), *Risk in intellectual and psychosocial development*. Orlando, FL: Academic Press.

Whisler, J. S. (1991). *The impact of the teacher on students' sense of self: A perspective from a model of mental health*. Aurora, CO: Mid-Continent Regional Educational Lab. (ERIC Document Reproduction Service No. ED 358394)

Whitaker, R. (1989, July 19). Parents get more day-care help at job. *Times Union*, p. A–1.

Whitbeck, L. B, & Simons, R. L. (1990). Life in the streets: The victimization of runaway and homeless adolescents. *Youth and Society*, 22(1), 108–125.

Whitebook, M., Howes, C., Phillips, D, & Pemberton, C. (1989). Who cares? Child care teachers and the quality of care in America. *Young Children*, 45(1), 41–45.

Wingert, P., & Kantrowitz, B. (1990, Winter/Spring). The day-care generation. *Newsweek*, Vol. CXIV(27), pp. 86–92.

Witkin, G., Hedges, S. J., Johnson, C., Guttman, M., Thomas, L., & Arrate, M. A. (1991, April 18). Kids who kill. *U.S. News and World Report*, pp. 26–32.

Wodarski, J. S., Hamblin. R. L., Buckholdt, D. R., & Ferritor, D. E. (1973). Individual consequences versus different shared consequences contingent on the performance of low-achieving group members. *Journal of Applied Social Psychology*, 3(3), 276–290.

Wolff, R. P. (1977). Understanding Rawls: A reconstruction and critique of a theory of justice. Princeton: Princeton University Press.

Wolins, M., & Gottesmann, M. (Eds.). (1971). *Group care: An Israeli approach: The educational path of Youth Aliyah*. New York: Gordon & Breach.

Woolfolk, A. (1990). *Educational Psychology*. New York: Prentice Hall.

Work in America (1981). Report of a special task force to the Secretary of Health, Education and Welfare. Cambridge, MA: MIT Press.

World Organization of Jews From Arab Countries (1987, October). Judicial Hearings before the Panel of the Legitimate Rights and Claims of Jews from Arab Countries. Washington, D.C.

Wrightsman, L. S. (Ed.) (1977). *Social psychology*. Monterey, CA: Brooks/Cole.

Yarrow, L. J (1961). Maternal deprivation: Toward an empirical and conceptual re-evaluation. *Psychological Bulletin*, 58, 459–490.

Zeskind, P. S., & Ramey, C. T. (1981). Preventing intellectual and interactional sequelae of fetal malnutrition: A longitudinal, transaction, and synergistic approach to development. *Child Development*, *52*, 231–218.

Zigler, E., & Hall, N. W. (1989). Day care and its effects on children: An overview for pediatric health professionals. *Annual Progress in Child Psychiatry and Child Development*, 543–560.

Zigler, E., & Trickett, P. K. (1978). IQ, social competence, and evaluation of early childhood intervention programs. *American Psychologist*, *33*, 789–798.

Index

Ability, 21, 23, 25, 29, 37–39, 41, 61, 66, 79, 86, 93, 100. *See also* Talent
Abolish the family, 34, 35, 44, 45
Abuse and neglect, 14, 15, 16, 23–25, 33, 47, 49, 72, 90; sexual, 15, 16, 90, 93, 94
Achievement, 41, 62, 63, 83, 92; individual vs. group, 83
Achievers, top vs. low, 61, 63, 64, 93
Aggression, 94, 95, 100, 101
Ainsworth, Mary, D., 95, 120 n.66
Alienation, 49, 65, 72, 80
Allen–Hagen, Barbara, 16, 90
Altruism, 4, 5, 95
Anomie, 11, 43, 66, 67, 69, 72, 102
Antisocial, 18, 83, 94. *See also* Aggression
Aries, Philippe, 19, 24
Attachment, 43, 47–51, 53, 56, 57, 59, 69, 72, 73, 75, 76, 95–97. *See also* Bowlby; Quality of, 95–99
Autonomous, 4, 84; behavior, 50, 57, 80, 98; choice, 21; decision making, 20, 21, 101; morally, 30, 80, 87. *See also* Independent
Autonomy, 4, 47, 20, 73, 74, 99, 100

Bargaining: model, 8, 10–12; strategy, 8
Belsky, Jay, 95, 120n.66
Benevolence, 4, 5

Bettelheim, Bruno, 58, 61, 63, 66, 73–75, 79
Better-off, 9–11, 32, 35, 43
Bias for justice. *See* Justice
Bond, 21, 47, 48, 56, 59, 69, 72, 78, 85, 96, 101. *See also* Social bond
Bowlby, John, 49, 50, 95

Capitalist society, 30, 31, 39, 43, 44
Caregiver, 96–100
Caretakers, 49, 94
Charvet, John, 34
Chevrot Nohar program. *See* Youth *Aliyah* program
Child homicide, 15, 18, 90
Child rearing: communal, 39, 44, 63, 82, 98; practices, 16, 23, 25, 46, 47, 49, 55, 87, 96, 99. *See also* Kibbutz, child rearing
Commitment, 5, 10, 11, 39, 47, 57, 61, 65, 69, 72, 73, 76, 78, 85; individual vs. group, 86
Common assets, 12, 37, 38, 42
Communication, 50, 51, 61, 78, 99–101
Community, 27, 38, 43, 45, 59, 72, 74, 98, 101; feeling of, 76; sense of, 38, 76, 83, 85, 86
Conflicts, 30, 6, 56, 73–77, 84, 86, 100
Conformity, 47, 48, 67, 73, 80; stake in, 49, 57, 59, 69, 73

Constraints: economic, 28; on
    liberty, 28; of the original position,
    1, 2, 4, 5, 10
Controls, 55, 93, 99; indirect, 55;
    self, 96, 98, 101; social, 3, 14, 47,
    48, 55, 58, 59, 61, 69
Cooperation, 5, 8, 9–11, 30, 37–41, 43,
    44, 57, 61, 63, 75, 76, 83–86,
    89, 100; vs. competition, 42, 83,
    84, 99–101
Crime, 11, 15, 18, 27, 69, 72, 90, 93

Day care, 28, 57, 94–102
Decision making: ability, 20, 21;
    procedure, 1, 13, 39, 43, 98
Delinquency, 16–19, 47–49, 61, 68, 69,
    72, 101; orientation to, 66, 67,
Delinquent, 16, 18, 19, 49, 61, 69, 72,
    85, 90, 102; activity, 65; acts,
    47–49, 55 61, 65, 69, 73
Democratic principles, 84, 86
Devereux, Edward, C., 56, 58, 74, 75,
    86, 87
Deviance, 17, 47, 48, 51, 55, 67, 65;
    cost of, 57, 67
Difference principle, 7–11, 22–25,
    27–29, 31–33, 38–40, 42, 45, 46,
    62, 64, 77, 78, 102
Disadvantaged, 14, 29, 40, 81, 82, 86,
    97
Discipline, 49, 56, 58, 93, 95, 101
Disintegrated families, 14, 45, 94
Divorce, 13–15, 72, 92
Dropouts, 16, 35, 61, 72, 93
Drug Abuse, 16, 66, 72, 90, 91, 93, 94,
    101
Durkheim, Emile, 69, 72, 76
Dysfunctional families, 14, 96, 102

Education, 20–22, 24, 32, 33–35, 37,
    40, 41, 44, 46, 61, 62, 64, 78, 83,
    92, 93, 101; communal, 44–46,
    56, 57, 61–64, 73, 74, 76,
    84–86, 102
Efficiency, 5, 31, 33, 83
Effort, 41, 42, 62, 96
Egalitarian relations, 30, 44, 76, 84, 101
Egoist, 76. See also Self-interest

Eiferman, Rivka, 83, 84, 87
Encouragement, 25, 33, 45, 62, 64, 83,
    84, 99, 100
Envious, 5, 6, 8
Envy, 11, 43, 76
Equal liberty principle, 7, 9, 38, 40
Equality, 9, 38, 43, 44, 59, 76, 79;
    of opportunity, 33–35, 37, 38

Fair(ness), 1, 3, 6, 11, 31, 33, 35, 38,
    40, 45, 56, 63, 64, 77, 85
Fair equality of opportunity, 7, 22, 24,
    33, 45, 46; principle of, 9, 10, 22,
    32, 34, 37, 40–42, 101
Feeling, of belonging, 43, 73
Fraternity, 11, 38
Free enterprise, 30, 31. See also
    Capitalist society
Freedom, 18, 20, 22, 27, 28, 40
Friends, 50–58, 61, 67, 73, 86, 94.
    See also Peer Group

In re Gault, 17–19
General assembly, 40, 41, 84, 85
Gewirth, Alan, 6, 21, 22
Gilligan, Carol, 79, 82, 87
Groups, 5, 18, 39, 41, 43, 44, 57, 62, 69,
    72–74, 78, 79, 83, 84, 86, 101;
    autonomous, 43; peer, 49, 57–59,
    73, 74, 76, 86, 101; performance,
    61–64, 83, 100; pressure, 58, 85,
    101; work, 64

Hirschi, Travis, 27, 47–51, 55, 57, 59,
    61, 65–67, 69, 78
Homeless, 16, 91, 92
Hume, David, 2, 5

Identification, 18, 50, 40, 51, 57, 75
Income supplement, 31, 33, 42
Incompetence, 20, 100
Incompetent parents, 23, 56
Independent, 57, 76, 95, 99. See also
    Autonomous
Individuality, 30, 73–76, 86
Indoctrination, 20, 73, 85
Inequalities, 1, 7–10, 25, 27, 46; of
    wealth and power, 27–31

Intimacy, 51, 73, 76
Intuition, 6, 8, 10, 11
Involvement, 61, 65, 98
Isolation, 42, 43, 65, 66, 79, 94

Jealousy, 76. *See also* Envy
Justice, 2, 3, 5–8, 10, 11, 30, 31, 36, 38,
    39, 41, 48, 66, 67, 77, 82, 85–87,
    89; bias for, 10–12; circumstances
    of 2, 7; as fairness, 3, 35, 64;
    principles of, 1, 2, 4–10, 12–14,
    27, 34, 38, 78; problem of, 6
Juvenile justice system, 16–19, 27

Kibbutz, 38–45, 89; child rearing, 39,
    46, 49, 63, 82, 87, 100. *See also*
    Education, communal; Child rearing.
    family, 40, 45; nurseries, 44, 98,
    100; pioneers, 38, 39, 44, 62;
    sleeping arrangements, 45, 49, 57,
    76; work(ers), 39, 40, 43–45, 62
Kibbutz vs. nuclear-family children,
    47, 49–71, 73–76, 79–84, 87
Kohlberg, Lawrence, 76–82, 85–87,
    101
Kozol, Jonathan, 91, 92

Labeling: criminals, 18; theories, 17
Least advantaged, 1, 7, 9–11, 24, 25, 40
    29–32; children, 16, 24, 25, 35,
    62–64, 91, 92, 102
Liberty, 7–9, 14, 18–20, 23, 28, 29, 38,
    40; exercise of, 21, 28, 29; rights,
    21, 23; worth of, 28–30
Locke, John, 20, 21, 24
Loco parentis, 17, 21

Madsen, Millard, 83, 84, 87, 119n50
Maximin strategy, 8, 9
Mead, Margaret, 56
Metapelet, 50, 56, 57, 84
Michaelman, Frank, 21–23
Miller, Richard, W., 11
Minimum wage, 31, 33
Moral: autonomy, 30, 47, 80, 87;
    behavior, 80, 86; Maturity Scores,
    80–82; persons, 2–4;
    thinking, 79, 80, 86, 87;

Moral*(continued)*; validity of
    social norms, 48, 66, 67, 69
Moral development, 13, 30, 47, 56, 73,
    76–82, 85, 100; Stages of, 48, 77,
    78, 80
Most advantaged, 10, 11, 35, 37, 38,
    64, 78
Mutual disinterest, 4, 5, 10, 78
Mutual: help, 38, 40, 83, 86, 100; aid,
    40, 43, 59

Natural abilities, 3, 25, 30, 37, 38.
Nature vs. nurture controversy, 25,
    38
Neglect. *See* Abuse and neglect
Nielsen, Kai, 34, 35, 45
Normative behavior, 48
Normless, 66. *See also* Anomie
Norms, 14, 18, 44, 48, 49, 66, 67, 69,
    72, 79, 80, 82, 85, 100
Nozick, Robert, 10, 33
Nuclear family, 14, 15, 25, 33, 35, 44,
    45, 89, 92
Nuclear-family vs. kibbutz children.
    See Kibbutz vs. nuclear-family
    children

One-parent homes, 92, 93, 96
Opportunity, 21–23, 28, 41, 45, 65,
    85–87, 100
Original position, 1–4, 6–11, 13,
    21–24, 29, 37, 38, 43, 47, 63, 77,
    79; constraints of the, 1, 2, 10;
    individuals in, 1–4, 6, 8, 9

Parens patria doctrine, 17, 19, 21
Participation, 27, 29, 38–41, 43, 44, 57,
    76, 78, 84, 86, 87, 101
Paternalism, 20, 21; paternalistic
    agencies, 24
Peer group, 43, 49, 56–59, 64, 74, 76,
    77, 85, 86, 90, 91, 95, 101;
    education, 57, 73; pressure, 58;
    socialization, 76. *See also* Groups;
    Friends
Peffer, Rodney, 22, 23
Performance, 93; individual vs. group,
    62–64, 84, 100

Person, model of, 2, 7; notion of, 3, 4
Piaget, Jean, 48, 49, 77
Plato, 45, 76, 77
Play, 58, 66, 83, 84, 95, 100, 101
Police, 27, 47, 59, 61
Poor families, 92, 93, 96
Poor vs. rich, 27–29, 32, 33, 35, 89, 96
Primary goods, 2–6, 8, 9, 21, 22, 24, 27,
    29, 31, 37, 39, 42, 47; theory of, 2,
    4
Profit, 30, 40, 75
Protection, 3, 10, 13, 14, 17–23
Punishment, 19, 35, 50, 56, 69, 79

Rabin, Albert, I., 50, 56, 63, 75, 76, 87
Rational reconstruction model, 6, 7,
    10, 11
Rawls, John, 1–13, 20–25, 27–34, 37,
    38, 41–45, 48, 49, 55–57, 59, 63–67
    77–79, 83–87, 102
Reciprocity, 11, 38, 57, 77, 79, 85
Redl, Fritz, 65
Reflective equilibrium, 6, 7, 10–12, 78
Reform, 1, 23, 31, 33, 35
Rejection, 50, 53, 57, 58, 94, 95, 99
Relative deprivation, 23, 29–33
Relative differences, 29, 42
Resources, 2, 11, 13, 22, 29, 30, 64;
    psychological and intellectual, 33,
    46
Respect, 3, 12, 33, 48, 57, 99
Rewards, 1, 37, 39, 41, 42, 57, 62, 64,
    65, 79, 83, 84, 100
Riesman, David, 66
Risktakers, 8, 22, 29
Roletaking, 11, 78, 79, 82, 86, 101
Rousseau, Jean-Jacques, 86
Runaways, 16, 93

Sartre, Jean-Paul, 44
Scarcity of goods, 2, 5, 8
School, 15, 16, 28, 33–35, 45, 48, 57,
    61–64, 77, 90, 91, 93–95, 100–102
Self-actualize, 12, 43
Self-control, 96, 99, 101
Self-esteem, 29, 38, 64, 85, 93–95, 99,
    102
Self-interest, 1, 4, 10, 67, 84

Self-interested (individual), 1, 4, 6, 10,
    48, 78
Self-respect, 3, 9, 21–23, 25, 27, 29,
    30, 31, 33, 38, 43, 47, 62
Self-worth, 3, 25, 43, 102
Selfish(ness) 5, 69
Sexual abuse, 15, 90, 93, 94
Shapira, Ariella, 83, 84, 87
Sharing, 11, 37, 38, 43, 50–52, 57, 84
Sleeping arrangement, 45, 49, 57, 76
Social bond, 39, 42, 45, 47, 48, 69, 78
Social disintegration, 11, 14, 72
Social minimum, 22, 31, 32
Social union, 12, 38, 43, 83
Socialist society, 30, 39, 42, 43
Socialization, 18, 47–49, 63, 64, 66, 74,
    76, 80
Socioeconomic goods, 7–9, 39, 42, 45
Solidarity, 39, 42, 43, 57, 85, 86
Spiro, Melford, E., 56
Sroufe, L. Alan, 96, 97
Standard of living, 24, 29, 31, 32, 42,
    44
Stepchildren, 93, 94
Stigma, 19, 33
Suicide, 11, 69, 72
Superego, 58, 74, 75
Supervision, 55, 56, 58
Support, 25, 33, 35, 38, 45, 50, 53, 54,
    56, 57, 63, 75, 97, 100

Talent(ed), 2, 11, 12, 21, 25, 37, 38, 41,
    42, 43, 61, 64.
Teenage mothers, 92–94
A Theory of Justice (Rawls), 5, 7, 8, 25,
    38, 78, 87
Trouble, 53, 54, 56, 57
Trust, 91, 99

Underachievers, 61, 92
Underprivileged, 45, 82, 101, 102
Unfairness, 33, 45, 56, 85
Uniqueness, 44, 73, 75, 76

Veil of ignorance, 2–8, 10, 11, 13, 78
Violence, 15, 90, 91, 93, 99, 101
Vocational training, 62, 64, 65, 101,
    102

Welfare rights, 22, 23
Well-being, 7, 16, 22, 90
Well-ordered society, 3, 7, 11, 23–25,
    30, 31, 33, 34, 37, 38, 41, 42, 45,
    59, 87
Women's employment, 15, 44, 94–98
Work, 31, 43, 44, 57, 62, 64–66, 84, 98,
    101, 102
Working parents, 55, 94, 96, 98
Worse-off, 9, 11, 24, 43

Youth *Aliyah/Chevrot Nohar* program,
    45, 81, 82, 86
Youth Society, 50, 57, 84–86, 101

About the Authors

BRENDA GEIGER, educational psychologist and philosopher, and MICHAEL FISCHER, criminal justice researcher and social scientist, have written on child development and delinquency issues. Their recent publications include *Reform through Community* (Greenwood Press, 1991) and two journal articles: "A Model for Change Following the Kibbutz Resocialization Program" (1994) and "Stimulating Moral Growth in the Classroom: A Model" (1994).

ISBN 0-313-29458-5

EAN

9 780313 294587

HARDCOVER BAR CODE